2 ⁰⁰⁄₃₋₁₉

AFTERGLOW

AFTERGLOW

A Last Conversation with
Pauline Kael

FRANCIS DAVIS

Da Capo Press
A Member of the Perseus Books Group

Designed by Jeffrey P. Williams
Set in 12-point Cochin by the Perseus Books Group

Cataloging-in-Publication data for this book is available from the
Library of Congress.

First Da Capo Press paperback edition 2003
First Da Capo Press edition 2002
ISBN 0–306–81230–4

Published by Da Capo Press
A Member of the Perseus Books Group
http://www.dacapopress.com

Da Capo Press books are available at special discounts for bulk purchases in
the U.S. by corporations, institutions, and other organizations. For more
information, please contact the Special Markets Department at the Perseus
Books Group, 11 Cambridge Center, Cambridge, MA 02142, or call (800)
255-1514 or (617) 252-5298, or e-mail j.mccrary@perseusbooks.com.

1 2 3 4 5 6 7 8 9—06 05 04 03

for
Sydney Goldstein

CONTENTS

INTRODUCTION

༈

IT WAS SATURDAY NIGHT and we had a date. Assuming we didn't have to wait too long for a table, dinner would be at the Union Bar and Grill on Main Street, where Pauline liked the portobello mushroom sandwich and where we had eaten lunch that afternoon. Picking a movie was trickier. Pauline explained that some smaller films came to Great Barrington a few weeks late. "But I know that *The Virgin Suicides*, the movie by Coppola's daughter, started yesterday," she said, reaching for the newspaper and her bifocals to see what else was playing at the Triplex and Hoyts. "I heard it doesn't have much story. What have you heard?"

I told her I'd seen it the weekend before, in Philadelphia.

"And?" Pauline wanted to know. "Is it anything?"

Since Pauline's retirement from *The New Yorker* in 1991, there had been a gradual change in our telephone conversations. Now that she was seeing fewer movies, I often found myself recommending new ones to *her*. Even so, it felt preposterous to be standing there describing a movie to Pauline Kael in her own living room. But I knew she expected a straight answer. (You never knew if, in asking your opinion of a movie, Pauline was testing you—measuring you by your taste.) I told her the movie wasn't as rich as the Jeffrey Eugenides novel it was based on. There were problems with the point-of-view, which the voice-over by Giovanni Ribisi did nothing to solve, even though it was straight from the book. And except for a scene where the boys sneak into the Lisbon family's house through a bathroom window and get turned on sniffing the daughters' toiletries and cosmetics, the script never approximated the voyeuristic rapture of Eugenides's prose. But the actresses who played the four Lisbon sisters were lovely, and Sofia Coppola had an eye for the sensual. Her movie was worth seeing.

A little more than a year later, when Pauline died, the reviews of hers that were mentioned most frequently in the newspaper obituaries were the ones where she intervened on behalf of movies in which she sensed greatness and that she worried might not find the audiences they deserved — *Nashville* and *Last Tango in Paris* being the most celebrated examples. But no one knew better than the author of *Movie Love* that loving movies meant asking more of them than they could routinely deliver. She wasn't going to be put off by my mixed review. *The Virgin Suicides* it was — but only for her. She didn't get the point of seeing a movie more than once. Everyone knew about this idiosyncrasy of hers; it was one of the things she was famous for during her reign as the queen bee of American movie critics, beginning with the publication of *I Lost It at the Movies* in 1965. It was also one of the ways in which we were different. What surprised me was her failure to comprehend why anyone else would be willing to sit through a movie a second time. Having talked about *The Virgin Suicides* in some detail for close to five minutes, I was actually looking forward to seeing it again, if only to check my memory for accuracy. But Pauline wouldn't hear of it. Dismissing my offer as unsolicited gallantry, she gave me a look that reminded me of the tone she'd once taken with me on the telephone when, knowing that she hadn't been feeling well, I suggested that she forget that letter of recommendation she'd offered to write for me. "Don't be an ass," she'd said, and that seemed to be what she was saying now.

We agreed to take a taxi into town, eat together, then part company at the box office. Pauline would go to *The Virgin Suicides*, and I would see *Chicken Run*, which started fifteen minutes later and was the only other movie playing, of the ones I hadn't seen, that I could work up any enthusiasm for. (The alternatives were *The Perfect Storm* and *Scary Movie 2*.) Whoever's movie ended first would wait for the other in the lobby, and we would use my cell phone to call Pauline's daughter Gina James, who lived just a couple blocks from the theater and could drive us back to Pauline's.

With that settled, Pauline said she could use a nap. I decided to take a walk into town to a used book store that Pauline said was a good place to browse. They were predicting rain for later that afternoon and it was already drizzling, so I asked Pauline if I could borrow one of the umbrellas she kept by the door in the shed. "But take another one," she said, as I opened one that turned out to be decorated with *The New Yorker*'s logo. "That one I never use. If they see you with that in town, they're going to think you're one of those pushy New Yorkers who come up here for the summer."

After dinner the night before, I'd gone for a walk with Sydney Goldstein of City Arts & Lectures, who had hired me to interview Pauline for her public radio series and had stayed for the first day of taping. It had still been light out when Sydney and I started up Berkshire Heights with no particular destination in mind, but had turned dark by the time we attempted to find our way back. Sydney, who lives in San Francisco, is as much a city creature as I am; the family we thumbed a ride with, and who got us safely back to Pauline's, laughed when Sydney told them that the house we were looking for was "on the corner." (The way to describe it would have been to say that the house was at the beginning of the road, hidden behind tall trees.) On my own now, I found my way to the book store with no trouble, but got hopelessly lost on the way back. I must have walked a mile out of my way, and just when I gained my bearings it began to pour. I was soaked by the time I reached Pauline's porch and opened the screen door, and it was obvious that we wouldn't be going anywhere that night.

That was all right with Pauline. She'd had groceries delivered just yesterday, and she felt like cooking anyway. Directors were always sending videos of their new movies, and there were plenty she hadn't watched yet, so we could watch one after dinner. And *Sex and the City* was on that night—a repeat of an episode from earlier that week, in which Carrie tries to quit smoking to please her new boyfriend. Pauline had already watched it, but she could catch up on her reading while I watched it. Staying home would be fun.

We chopped vegetables and thawed chicken breasts in the microwave as we listened to reports of flooded roads and downed power lines on the portable black-and-white television on the kitchen counter. Pauline's grandson, Will, who was home from college and living with her for the summer, bounded into the kitchen and announced he wouldn't be eating at home; it would take more than what the television was calling the worst storm in southwestern Massachusetts in fifty years to keep a teenager home on a Saturday night. (He postponed his departure a half-hour or so on learning that I'd never seen *Black Adder*, a comedy series that traces British history from the fifteenth to the early twentieth century through the mishaps of a long line of wretches, all played by Rowan Atkinson. Dragging me into the living room so he could play me one of his favorite episodes, Will shrieked with delight at the best jokes, loudly repeating many of them in a fake British accent.)

Setting the dining room table involved clearing it of the many screenplays that had recently been sent to Pauline by writers seeking her advice or courting her approval. Maybe it was the sight of so many screenplays that reminded her of the first time she read Paul Schrader's script for *Taxi Driver*. She was in New York, staying overnight at the Royalton, the hotel across from the *New Yorker* offices, when Schrader dropped it off. It was late and she was tired, so she took the script to bed with her. She intended to read just the first few pages before turning off the light, but got so caught up in Travis Bickle's dementia that she read straight through to the end, putting the script on a night table when she finished. She tossed and turned and couldn't sleep—she felt the presence of something menacing in the room with her. She put the light on, reached beside her and turned the screenplay face down, and then slept like a baby.

We were startled by the sound of someone coming in the back door. "Who's there?" Pauline cried out in as loud a voice as she could muster. It was her old friend, the writer Roy Blount Jr., checking to make sure her electricity was still on and to see if she needed his help with anything. She assured him we were fine and invited him to have dinner with us, but he explained that he needed to get going, to check on his own house.

We went back to our salads, and Pauline told me that Schrader was still a devoted friend, despite the harsh notices she'd given the first few films he directed after writing *Taxi Driver* for Martin Scorsese ("Paul Schrader may like the idea of prostituting himself better than he likes making movies," she ended her review of *Hardcore*. "For Schrader to call himself a whore would be vanity: he doesn't know how to turn a trick."). A few years earlier, when she was hospitalized after a bad reaction to one of the drugs she was taking for her Parkinson's, she woke from a long, comalike sleep and there was

Schrader by her bedside. He'd driven up from New York when he heard she was sick and had been there several hours, waiting for her to regain consciousness.

After doing the dishes, we ran into the same problem we'd had that afternoon, when it looked like we'd be going out to a movie. There were dozens of videos around the house, but hardly any that neither of us had seen. I spotted Mike Hodges's *Croupier*, which I adored and would have been curious to hear what Pauline thought of. But I made the mistake of telling her that I had already seen it not once but twice. "Then I'm not going to force you to watch it again, just because I ought to see it," she said. "I can always watch it later." And that was the end of the discussion.

We wound up watching *Galaxy Quest*, a comedy starring Tim Allen and Sigourney Weaver. The movie's premise was that the humanlike inhabitants of a planet in a distant galaxy had somehow been exposed to reruns of a vintage television series about the adventures of a crew of idealistic space explorers. These aliens had mistaken the show for reality, and when their planet comes under attack, they seek the help of the cynical, washed-up cast members to defeat the invaders. To think, the day before Pauline had told me about going to see *Deep Throat*—watching Linda Lovelace taking it all in, as it were—with the novelist Charles Simmons. And here I was watching an innocent little *Star Trek* parody with her. Pauline enjoyed the movie much more than I did. "That's sweet," she said once or twice, when the head alien declared his undying loyalty to the principles of brotherhood espoused by the television series. She sucked cough drops to relieve the dry mouth caused by her blood pressure medication, and even with the soundtrack roaring and rain pelting the windows and mosquitoes buzzing under the light outside the screen door, I could hear them clicking against her teeth. She could have been anybody's ailing eighty-year-old granny. But then she would say something about a nice edit or one of the actors' previous roles and—she was Pauline Kael.

After *Sex and the City*, we watched an episode of *Oz*, one of my favorite shows. Pauline found it lurid and lost interest in it pretty quickly. "It's the same thing as those old Warner Brothers prison movies with James Cagney," she said, overlooking the male rape. Will returned around midnight and, after showing us how wet he was, made himself a snack and went to bed. By 2 A.M., I was fading and Pauline was still going strong. She was reading aloud to me from her protégé Elvis Mitchell's review of *X-Men* in the *Times*, but I was too sleepy to follow it. I kissed her goodnight and turned in.

No longer able to climb stairs without great difficulty, Pauline now slept in a guest room on the first floor, which meant that I could have the master bedroom where Sydney had slept the night before. This had been Pauline's bedroom, and it was connected by a sliding door to the large room that had been her office. By the windows in this second room were neatly arranged stacks of *The New Yorker* and *The New York Review of Books*, and I had the sensation that there were also original manuscripts and corrected galleys nearby. But I was too exhausted to snoop.

I woke early the next morning and showered and made coffee as quietly as I could, not wanting to wake anyone else. I tiptoed out to the porch to wait for my taxi to the airport in Albany. "Have a safe flight, sweetie," Pauline called after me from her bedroom as I gingerly opened the screen door.

I WISH I COULD REMEMBER everything Pauline told me over lunch and dinner that weekend. Some of it was livelier than anything on the tape we gave Sydney. I remember a story about her meeting Duke Ellington at a White House Conference on the Arts in 1965. She and Ellington struck up a conversation during the pre-dinner reception. They were seated at different tables for dinner, with Ellington next to Lady Bird Johnson. Following coffee and dessert, Ellington excused himself to the First Lady and strolled over to Pauline to resume their chat. A presidential aide caught up with him and explained that one doesn't leave the First Lady's table before she does. Ellington apologized for the breach in protocol and returned to his seat, but only after suggesting to Pauline that they meet later for drinks. She declined, because she had a flight to catch, she told me, and she still didn't know if Ellington was coming on to her—nor how she felt about it, if that was the case. She was both fascinated and repelled by him. The reception was on the White House lawn, and it was a humid and hazy afternoon. Ellington was still straightening his hair then, and though taken with his charm, all Pauline could think about, she said, was the pomade oozing from his scalp, along with the sweat.

She told me a lot I didn't know about her career, including that she was interviewed for a position as drama critic at the *New York Times* around 1966. "They brought me in as a formality, because a few very influential people told them they should consider me," she said. "They weren't really serious about me, and I wasn't going to take the job if they offered it to me." (The *Times* filled the vacancy with Stanley Kauffmann, which opened up a slot as movie critic at *The New Republic* for Pauline.) Contrary to legend, Pauline said, she wasn't fired by *McCall's* for panning *The Sound of Music* and dubbing it "The Sound of Money." According to Pauline, the magazine was tightening its belt and she was one of several writers whose contracts were not renewed.

She spoke freely about her worsening physical condition and diminished short-term memory. "I can go on for hours about a movie I saw decades ago, but not even remember the name of the one I saw yesterday," she warned me before we started taping. Years ago in New York, she said, when she would go out to dinner with Elvis Mitchell, who is African-American and wears his hair in dreadlocks,

and it was his turn to pay, the waiter would invari-
ably return his credit card to Pauline's side of the
table without looking at the name. Now, when she
had visitors and took them to a restaurant and paid
with her credit card, the waiter would hand the card
to anyone but her, assuming that she was too addled
to be trusted with one. Perhaps the most surprising
thing she told me concerned her hallucinations a
few years earlier, when her doctors put her on l-dopa
to combat her Parkinson's symptoms. These hallucinations, of lions and tigers ripping her flesh and
crunching through bone, were especially terrifying
because she'd never experienced anything remotely
like them. It turns out that Pauline, for all her love
of trippy movie imagery and despite a writing style
that could be like an amphetamine rush, had never
done drugs — not even in the late 1960s, when it was
impossible for her to go to a party without someone
offering to turn her on. "I liked having my wits
about me," she explained, adding with what I
thought was a trace of humor, "Movies were
enough."

My formal interview with Pauline, which was
conducted over two days in July 2000 (and has
been chronologically rearranged here), was Sydney

Goldstein's idea. In addition to presenting speakers at various locations around San Francisco, her City Arts & Lectures also produces a nationally distributed radio program. Most episodes of this program, including an earlier one with Pauline from a few years ago, are culled from the organization's live events. Syndey wanted an encore from Pauline, and since Pauline was in no condition to travel, the only way to get her was to go where she was. Sydney and Pauline talked by phone every so often, as did Pauline and I, and more than once she had invited each of us to visit her at home in Great Barrington, Massachusetts. Both Sydney and I are comically insecure, and when someone you know mostly from the telephone issues a casual invitation, you're never sure if you're supposed to take him or her up on it. I think both of us felt safer barging in on Pauline for the first time in the professional roles of interviewer and producer. Sydney was edgy on the ride from the airport; her mother had died from Parkinson's, she said, and she was afraid of the painful memories that the sight of a diminished Pauline might bring back. She was relieved as soon as we saw Pauline waving to our taxi from her screen door. The tremor in her voice had grown more pronounced since I last spoke with her, only a few weeks earlier, and she couldn't go very far without her cane. But her voice was still merry, and she was still the Pauline we remembered and admired, tart and crackling with energy as she gave us the grand tour, showing us the exercise bike she said she hardly ever used, the Tiffany lamps she had picked up cheap over the years, the paintings by her friend Manny Farber, the white piano that had once belonged to the visual artist Jess, and the shelf of foreign translations of her books.

If my questions to Pauline occasionally sound like those of a sycophant, so be it. Surely everybody knows by now that the father of her daughter, Gina James, was not one of Pauline's three husbands, but the poet James Broughton, who was gay. Wanting a child, Pauline entered into an arrangement with Broughton that would not be so unusual today, but represented a bold step for a woman in the 1950s. It was I, not Pauline, who put such personal matters out of bounds. I wanted to talk with her writer-to-writer, and I wish I had asked her more about craft. Writing always involves an element of self-delusion, and Pauline apparently was no exception to the rule. To hear her talk, you would think that, after writing a review in a burst and handing it in, she went through galleys carefully, undoing the damage done by William Shawn and *The New Yorker*'s other editors until the piece conformed to what she had written in the first place. I don't doubt that she believed this, but according to Bill Whitworth, who was one of Pauline's editors at *The New Yorker* and mine at *The Atlantic Monthly*, this wasn't quite how the process would go. Bill says that Pauline would indeed suggest many changes to the galleys — but that much of what she penciled in consisted of thoughts not in her original manuscript, not all of them in response to editorial queries. This would have been something to confront her with, and there are readers (myself among them) who never tire of hearing about the inner workings of *The New Yorker* under Shawn. But because ours was an interview in lieu of the talk that Pauline might have given for City Arts & Lectures if she had been able to travel, I saw my role as being her sounding board. Given this, I probably shouldn't have ventured as many opinions as I did during our talk. My only defense is to point out that if it's difficult to interview someone you hold in awe, it's even harder to conduct a formal interview with someone you're used to chatting with on the telephone every so often. Such an interview is eventually going to lapse into a conversation, and this one certainly did. But that's all right; I hope it gives this book some flavor.

Though I had read *I Lost It at the Movies* as a college freshman soon after it was published, my personal relationship with Pauline began in 1987, when I wrote her a fan letter and enclosed a copy of my first book (a collection of essays on jazz), along with a timid request for a blurb that could be used on the paperback. I had no reason to believe that Pauline read much jazz criticism, but one piece of hers in particular demonstrated a keen understanding of the forces at work in jazz, and this was enough to give me hope. "Pop music provides immediate emotional gratifications that the subtler and deeper and more lasting pleasures of jazz can't prevail against," she wrote in her review of *Lady Sings the Blues* in 1972:

Pop drives jazz back underground. And that's what this pop movie does to the career of a great jazz singer. . . .

Billie Holiday expressed herself in her bantering with lachrymose lyrics, making them ironic and biting, or else exploiting them for their full measure of misery, giving in so deeply to cheap emotions that she wrung a truth of her own out of them.

A few weeks later, a handwritten letter arrived from Pauline on *New Yorker* stationary and in one of those RSVP-size envelopes the magazine went on using well into the Robert Gottlieb administration:

Dear Francis Davis,

Will this do for a quote?

He's a very impressive critic. He doesn't pin fancy phrases on his chest; he gets at what he responds to and why—you feel you're reading an honest man.

Best,
Pauline Kael

My publisher was delighted, needless to say, but I was close to being paralyzed. For about six months, I couldn't write a declarative sentence without worrying whether I was being "honest." The following spring, my wife and I attended a New

York critics' screening of Wim Wenders's *Wings of Desire* that let out at the same time as a screening of Dennis Hopper's *Colors* in another room on the same floor. We saw Pauline walking out of *Colors* and putting on her coat, and before I could work up the nerve to go over and introduce myself, she came over to me and asked if I was Francis Davis. (She recognized me from my jacket photo.) We exchanged phone numbers, and she called a few weeks later to tell me she enjoyed a piece I had written about the singer Bobby Short for *7 Days*. That call broke the ice, and we would talk every so often—about movies, naturally, but since I always seemed to be asking her for career advice, the topic of our conversation was often me. As if for the same reason that some devout Jews will not utter the name of Yahweh—God is unnameable—*New Yorker* writers rarely refer to their publication by name. They call it "the magazine." Now and then, Pauline would ask me, with some exasperation, "When are you going to write a piece for the magazine?" making it seem like the choice was mine. She talked as if I were her equal, and no one has ever paid me a sweeter compliment.

IN 1944, W. H. AUDEN wrote a letter to *The Nation* in which he said that James Agee's film reviews were the first thing he turned to every week, even though he rarely went to the movies. Pauline likewise heard all too often that her reviews were frequently more stimulating than the movies that served as her point of departure. In a way, there's no greater insult for a critic: It's saying, "I love you, but I will not surrender to your passion." Still, in Pauline's case, it was sometimes true. No one else has written as vividly about movies, or about the experience of *seeing* movies. But she didn't blink when she left the movie theater and walked into the light. You can open any of her books at random, as I just did, and find novelistic insights like these, from her review of a forgettable 1976 movie called *Sparkle*, with Lonette McKee as Sister, "a rebellious, nose-thumbing" soul singer who "falls for [a] sadistic pusher who beats her up and degrades her":

> The subject that's passed over—why the thug wants to possess and destroy Sister, who so obviously has everything it takes to become a star, and why she's drawn to him—is a true

modern subject, and not just for the rock world. Lonette McKee is the actress to drive the theme into one's consciousness, because she has the sexual brazenness that screen stars such as Susan Hayward and Ava Gardner had in their youth. You look at the sheer taunting sexual avidity of these women and you think "What man would dare?" And the answer may be: only a man with the strength to meet the challenge or a man so threatened by it that he's got to wipe the floor with the girl, and there are more of the latter. If the women who are "too much" for men fall for sharpies and rough guys who brutalize them, it probably has to do with the scarcity of the other men, and something to do, too, with the women's insecurity about being too much. The stronger a woman's need to use her energy, her brains, her talent, the more con-fusedly she may feel that she has a beating coming. Besides, having had to make her own way, and having—at some levels—been coarsened doing it, she may feel some rapport with the tough operators who are used to knocking people around. Whatever else these men are, they're self-made, and they instinctively know what she's gone through and how to handle her.

Movies now seem to be almost begging for this theme to come out. It's highly unlikely that a woman can become a major screen star at this time unless she has a strong personality, yet if she does—like Jane Fonda, or Barbra Streisand, or Liza Minnelli—she's likely to be experienced as threatening by some of the audience (and by women who play by the standard rules as well as by men). These stars raise the problem in their relation to the audience which is implicit in their screen roles: resentment of their dominating presence. Yet at the movies audiences are far more interested in the "bad girls" than in the ingenues, and not just because wickedness gives an actress more of a chance; these roles give an actress a better chance because there's something recognizably there in those bad girls, even when it's frustrated, soured, and self-destructive. The "bad girl" is the cheapest, easiest way for the movies to deal with the woman with guts.

Was Pauline the most influential movie critic of her generation? The most influential ever? You could answer the question either way. Andrew Sarris and the French auteurists, not Pauline, were the ones who determined which directors belonged in the pantheon. But even though certified men and women of letters had turned their attention to the cinema as early as the 1940s, it was Pauline who established the movie review as a form of literature with the potential for social commentary. As zingy as their prose is, in futile emulation of hers, most of today's film critics have apparently learned nothing from her. They tend to be distressingly middlebrow, no different from those of their readers whose idea of a four-star movie is an updated woman's picture or a sodden problem drama. (These are the same people, and the same critics, who seem to think that European movies are "smarter" than ours because the characters in them speak a foreign language.) "[T]he educated audience often uses 'art' films in much the same self-indulgent way as the mass audience uses the Hollywood 'product,' finding wish fulfillment in the form of cheap and easy congratulation on their sensitivities and their liberalism," Pauline wrote in 1962, more than three decades before *The English Patient* started an art-house vogue for pseudo-intellectual bodice rippers. The problem with today's critics is that they're all the same person; with only a few exceptions (like Armond White of *The New York Press*), none of them has the independence—or the nerve—to go to bat for a good movie that's been given up for dead by its distributors, as Pauline did on so many occasions, including *Pennies from Heaven* and *Casualties of War*. I like to think that Pauline would agree with me that *All the Pretty Horses*, *Death to Smoochie*, and *The Princess and the Warrior* are better than *In the Bedroom*, *Monster's Ball*, and the laborious *Time Out*. But who knows? We disagreed about movies more often than our conversation here might lead you to believe, and I often wondered if she would have abided my disagreement so graciously were I a fellow movie critic, rather than someone who wrote mostly about jazz. By the same token, her influence on me as a writer has gone largely undetected, because my subject matter is different from hers. In being an un-outed Paulette, I am hardly alone among music writers; Pauline's insistence that art happens in the real world and that it should be an instrument of pleasure has become a governing

principle in writing about rock and pop. Her importance as a movie critic cannot be overestimated, but
it pales before her influence as a critic, period—and
as a writer.

I think the very last conversation I had with
her was soon after I was named a Senior Fellow for
2001–2002 by the National Arts Journalism
Program, at Columbia University, and she was
named the program's first Distinguished Lecturer
(a position specially created for her). My fellowship
required a three-month New York residency that
was waved for Pauline, although she was expected
to give a talk on campus some time during the
school year (or possibly speak by remote). She told
me her fellowship money would be going toward
her medical bills, which were becoming enormous.
She was far too ill to attend a party for the incom-
ing fellows in New York in late August, at which
her friend Craig Seligman (another 2001–2002
NAJP Senior Fellow) gave me a report on her condition in hushed tones, worried that we might say
something that would jeopardize her honorarium.
She died less than two weeks later, on Labor Day.

I miss her, of course, but I was luckier than
those readers who were forced to say good-bye to

her prematurely, on her retirement from *The New Yorker* eleven years earlier. Had *The New Yorker* been a different sort of magazine, it could have run a contest: "Win a Dream Date with Pauline Kael." Reading her was like going to the movies with someone you adored; when you disagreed with her, it was like having a lover's quarrel.

I think of this slim volume as a keepsake of my friendship with Pauline. Readers are invited to think of it as a keepsake of her remarkable literary career. There would be no book if not for the indefatigable Sydney Goldstein, who persuaded me that it would be a good idea to go talk to Pauline, and then persuaded me that there was more to the story than just the interview. Nathaniel Friedman helped me to prepare for the interview with his painstaking research, and much later in the game, Bill Alatriste helped me to track down the article in which François Truffaut referred to "the tradition of quality." Bill Whitworth, Carrie Rickey, and Craig Seligman, all of whom knew Pauline better and for much longer than I did, brought me closer to her by generously sharing their memories. A portion of the interview ran on *The New Yorker's* website a few weeks after Pauline's death; my thanks to David

Remnick, Pam McCarthy, Amy Tubke-Davidson, and Adam Shatz and the magazine's other fact checkers for their careful reading of the transcript and their perceptive suggestions. My NAJP fellowship gave me the luxury of working on this book and another simultaneously, without worrying about magazine deadlines. Thanks also to my father-in-law Irving Gross; my agent Mark Kelley; Andrea Schulz, who brought me to Da Capo Press; and John Radziewicz, who inherited me on Andrea's departure and proved to be as patient and insightful an editor as any writer could hope for. My mother Dorothy Davis, who died five months before Pauline, will always be an inspiration; she used to tell me whenever Pauline's name appeared in her crossword puzzle — information that delighted Pauline. And as usual, my greatest debt is to my wife, Terry Gross, who's taught me a thing or two about interviewing in the twenty-five years we've been together, along with so much else.

FRANCIS DAVIS
Philadelphia
May 2002

PART ONE

꒯

FRANCIS DAVIS: When you liked a movie, your enthusiasm was contagious. I was in college when Jean-Luc Godard's *Masculine-Feminine* came out in 1966, and though I desperately wanted to see it after reading your review in *The New Republic* and was up on the French new wave, it seemed out of the running because I was dating a girl who didn't like foreign movies — to begin with, she didn't like having to read subtitles. We had a class together on Monday mornings, where we sat next to each other, and I very carefully left the magazine on my desk, opened to your review. The plan worked. She read your review, and we saw *Masculine-*

Feminine that weekend — at her insistence, because she'd caught your fever. Anyway, my reason for telling the story is that I subsequently read this was one of the pieces that convinced William Shawn to bring you on at *The New Yorker*.

PAULINE KAEL: Yes. Godard was one of the reasons he hired me. William Shawn went to the movies often but rarely sat through an entire movie, because, he said, he couldn't stand brutality or bloodshed, and he would leave at the slightest hint of violence. So he saw the beginnings of a lot of movies, and he realized that there was something to Godard. I had been writing very lovingly about Godard, and Shawn was very unhappy that *The New Yorker*'s critics had been panning movie after movie by him for years.*

What surprises me is that your review of *Masculine-Feminine* was as much about the direc-

---

*In fact, several different *New Yorker* writers had reviewed Godard's early movies enthusiastically — though perhaps not as enthusiastically as Pauline thought they deserved. In any case, this is myth.

tor's relationship to youth culture as it was about the movie —

I was often accused of writing about everything but the movie.

It's just that one doesn't imagine William Shawn being very tuned in to youth culture in 1966.

He was interested in a surprising number of things. It's funny, because he took very dowdy attitudes toward what could appear in the magazine, but he himself was very alive and alert to all sorts of things. He often argued with me about how I shouldn't review a particular movie because it was brutal or dirty or one thing or another. He wanted some sort of censorship imposed, but he couldn't, rigorous man that he was, impose it. So he tried to talk the magazine's writers into censoring themselves, and I didn't go for that. But he went to see all sorts of things and was quite open in what he responded to. He followed Richard Pryor from the very beginning of his nightclub career, and when you consider how pristine the language in *The New Yorker* had to be, you'll see how remarkable it is that William Shawn enjoyed listening to Richard Pryor.

According to legend, the only movie he ever talked you out of reviewing was *Deep Throat*.

That's right. And I still feel that I should have put up more of a squawk, but I had gotten so tired of battling with him. Charlie Simmons has a passage about going to see that movie with me in his novel *Wrinkles*.* But I couldn't convince Shawn that a porn movie was worth writing about. He thought it was just some perversity on my part that I wanted to cover *Deep Throat*.

Did you think it was a good movie?

No, it wasn't a good movie. But I very badly wanted to write about it, because for all that was being written about it, nobody was really dealing with what

---

*From *Wrinkles* (1978): "She invited him soon after to see *Deep Throat*, giggled throughout, and was shushed by the men in the audience. As they were leaving the theater they walked through a narrow passage by the men's room; a burly, pimpled boy emerged and rubbed himself against her. She elbowed the boy in the chest and giggled."

was on the screen. I think half of the reason that people become interested in movies in the first place is sex and dating and everything connected with eroticism on the screen. And I felt that not to deal with all of that in its most naked form was to shirk part of what's involved in being a movie critic.

I'd love to have written more about eroticism in the movies. I think it's a great subject, and I dealt with it a little bit in my reviews of *Last Tango in Paris*, *Get Out Your Handkerchiefs*, and a few other movies. Bertrand Blier I loved writing about, because he dealt so much in sexual areas. But it was tough to write about it at all with Shawn. I had a real tough time with him when I wrote about *Tales of Ordinary Madness*, the Marco Ferreri version of Charles Bukowski, about a girl who's virtually a mermaid, with Ben Gazzara as Bukowski, more or less. It's an amazing movie, with some scenes that are quite erotic. I had to put up a terrible fight to get it in. Shawn wanted to know if the critics for other magazines were covering it. I said that shouldn't be our standard for what we covered in *The New Yorker*. But it was hard to convince Shawn that I wasn't pulling some sort of swindle by sneaking material into the magazine that he felt didn't belong there.

He felt he was holding the line against the barbarians, and to some degree I was a barbarian.

He made it very hard to write about certain aspects of movies. Nobody, really, has done a very good job of writing on a sustained level about the way movies affect people erotically, and about the fact that they became popular because they're a dating game. People love movies for that reason, because they excite them sexually. They go to them on dates, and they go to learn more about how to behave. I never got a real crack at writing about that. It was awful having to fight with Shawn, someone who was so revered and whom I admired. But I was writing about a popular art form, and the magazine had gotten a little stiff. So it was difficult.

Yeah. Middlebrow taste often mistakes itself for highbrow — that's practically a definition.

And I loved lowbrow taste, and that was hard to get across. One of the great things about movies is they can combine the energy of a popular art with the possibilities of a high art. What's wonderful about someone like Altman is that mixture of pop and high art. He's an artist who uses pop as his vehicle. That's part of the excitement in a movie like *Nashville*; you get a sense of the different forces at work on the director. Godard's *Weekend* is another case in point. It has that pop element, but the director is an artist who's using pop. Other arts don't have that in the way that movies and popular music do. It's why popular music excites us; and the best movies excite us in the same way.

When you started at *The New Yorker*, you wrote every week for six months and then gave way to another critic for the rest of the year. Was it ever suggested to you, by Shawn or anyone else, that you could use the hiatus to write about subjects other than movies?

Well, it was tricky. I had to go out and make a living for six months of the year, so I didn't have the luxury of sitting at home and working on a long piece. I had to go out and teach at UCLA or somewhere else, generally, because if I wrote about new movies it would be in conflict with what was being said in *The New Yorker*. A few times, I tried to work on pieces that I was unhappy with and threw out. I tried to write about television once. I worked on the piece for several weeks, and it was just awful. Television is hard to write about. I think that Jim Wolcott is one of the few people who ever licked the problem. I couldn't. Maybe if I had written about it week by week, as I did movies, I could have gotten the hang of it. But writing a big piece on television was a nightmare. It was just crap, and I threw it out. It wasn't easy adapting to another subject, in part because I was keeping up with the new movies and tormented by the ones I wanted to write about and couldn't.

There are times now that I wish I had branched off, but I also regret not writing much about certain directors—particularly Chris Marker, whose work I think is of considerable importance, and some of it is very exciting.* I didn't write about it because Terrence Rafferty was also at *The New Yorker*, and he was writing a book about Marker. And I thought Terry would publish more on Marker in the magazine.

I didn't write as much about Jacques Demy as I would have liked, either. I love *The Umbrellas of*

---

*A French documentary filmmaker regarded as one of the fathers of *cinema-vérité*. His films include *Description d'un Combat* and *Le Joli Mai*.

Cherbourg. One of the sad things about our times, I think, is that so many people find a romantic movie like that frivolous and negligible. They don't see the beauty in it, but it's a lovely film—original and fine. *The Young Girls of Rochefort,* Demy's other big musical, was a disaster, I think. The dancing in it is bad, and it just doesn't work. The other film of his that I love, along with *The Umbrellas of Cherbourg,* is *Bay of Angels,* with Jeanne Moreau as a gambling lady, like Barbara Stanwyck in some of her movies.

There were a lot of directors and a lot of actors I never really got a chance to write about, because you play it by ear in terms of what's opening this week or the week after, and the fact is that for my first twelve years at *The New Yorker,* I was only there six months a year, so I missed writing about a lot of movies that opened during my absence that I desperately wanted to write about. I never got a chance to talk about Altman's *California Split,* which is a terrific movie. People now assume that I didn't write about certain movies because I didn't think they merited it. They don't understand that there's a protocol at a magazine; you can't go butting into somebody else's turf too often. You have to be watchful and protective of other people's rights.

Did anyone at the magazine ever ask you why you were wasting your time reviewing movies one by one, as they came out, and encourage you to write longer think pieces about them?

No. But they thought I was awful for panning the kind of movies I panned, the earnest movies, what's now called the independent film—the movies that have few aesthetic dimensions but are moral and have lessons and all. There was a great deal of sentiment for that kind of movie at *The New Yorker*, and from its readers. This was, after all, in the sixties and seventies, and New York was still full of a lot of refugees from Hitler, and they took movies very seriously, and morally. And my frivolous tone really bugged them. Before that, when I wrote for *The New Republic*, the readers there were offended because they were used to Stanley Kauffmann. They thought of me as an impertinent snip and wrote hostile letters to the magazine, many of which were printed.

Today, there's so much more of a feeling for films as aesthetic objects rather than as morally improving objects. But I was writing for a magazine that stood for moral improvement—*New Yorker* editorials during my years there could be so abstractly moralizing. There were things there that were so at odds with what I was doing that it amazes me that I lasted.

Well, whatever else, Shawn recognized good writing.

He also recognized that I significantly lowered the average age of the magazine's readers. It was something the advertising department was very well aware of, too. You know, if you took away the homosexual audience from the arthouses, or the elderly Jewish audience from Carnegie Hall, you wouldn't have much left. And that's what was happening to *The New Yorker*: Its readership was dying off faster than Sol Hurok's customers.

Have you looked at any of the recent spate of books on *The New Yorker*?

I've looked at several of them, and the one by Ben Yagoda is quite good.* I recognize the magazine from the way he writes about it. I didn't recognize it

---

About Town (2000).

in some of the other books. I mean, I was dashing into the city from Great Barrington, turning in my copy, running out to screenings, coming back to the magazine to correct galleys, going to more movies, and then going home to write. Apparently, I missed all the intrigue going on at the magazine, because I witnessed very little of it, and when word did reach my ears I didn't pay much attention, because I didn't have the time. You can't spend all your time plotting against your fellow workers when you're turning in copy every week or every other week, as I did.

So I was stunned when that piece by Renata Adler came out in *The New York Review of Books* in which she rejected everything I had ever written.* I was told by Harold Brodkey that it was a group effort — that a dozen or so people helped out on it, in a group movement to denounce me. I knew nothing about it. I had no idea that it was coming, that anything was building. I was busy innocently going to the movies and writing about them.

---

*Adler, a colleague at *The New Yorker* and an occasional film critic herself, dismissed Kael's film criticism as "piece by piece, line by line, and without interruption, worthless."

Adler's piece was ostensibly a review of your latest collection, but it amounted to a vicious, ad hominem attack. I always thought the timing was significant: it ran right after you returned to *The New Yorker* from Hollywood, in 1980.

That's right. It greeted me.

Did Shawn ever say anything to you about it? *The New Yorker* was like a family, albeit an extremely dysfunctional one, and he was the father.

He indicated that he was upset and very pained about it. But you could never tell with William Shawn. He may have given the other people involved the impression that he sided with them. There's nothing like a devious editor to leave you hanging in the air.

As long as we're talking about Shawn and *The New Yorker*, there are a few other things I want to ask you about, if you don't mind telling tales of school.

I might mind when I hear what they are. But go ahead.

Everyone knows he objected to your use of what he considered crude language.

Right.

But you once told me that he also objected to your use of filmic terms that he thought might be too technical for a general readership. What were some of them?

Well, one of them would certainly have been *filmic*. And I agree with him on that one. I see no reason for that word. What the devil does it mean? But I honestly can't recall what the others were.

Did he ever think that something you said about an actor or director was too cruel? Like when you described Dyan Cannon as "looking a bit like Lauren Bacall and a bit like Jeanne Moreau, but the wrong bits"?

Dyan Cannon roared over that one, I'm happy to say. She's a very smart, very lively woman, and she was very sweet about it. I don't recall if Shawn objected to that, but that was the sort of thing he often did object to. He sometimes talked me out of things that I'm not sure he was right about, but I gave in, because I thought that maybe he was right. You know, sometimes you leave out things that seem part of the story you're telling, because you don't want to hurt people. That makes sense.

I'm happy to say that at least some of the people who objected to my review of *Shoah* have told me that they've since come to agree with me.* I had a rough time with that. It was the only time that Shawn held up my copy, that he didn't immediately print something I had turned in. I finally insisted that it had to be printed the following week, or nothing at all.

Shoah "is a long moan" Kael concluded her review of Claude Lanzmann's 1985 nine-hour documentary on the Nazi's Polish "death factories." "It's saying 'We've always been oppressed, and we'll be oppressed again.' . . . This is not necessarily an aberrant or irrational notion, and a moan is not an inappropriate response to the history of the Jews. But the lack of moral complexity in Lanzmann's approach keeps the film from being a great moan. When you're watching [Marcel Ophuls's *The Sorrow and the Pity*], your perspective expands: you keep changing your mind, and you can see that [Ophuls is] changing his, too. You don't just become self-righteous about gloating, mean-spirited peasants and unfeeling Nazi bureaucrats. . . . [*Shoah*] is exhausting to watch because it closes your mind."

Shoah was one of those movies that was tricky, because not liking it meant that you were accused of being insensitive to the Holocaust.

That's right, and the Holocaust was something that readers of *The New Yorker* were very sensitive about—as they were about *Rain Man* and other movies about illnesses. I once got a letter from a woman telling me I was irresponsible for saying anything good about a Woody Allen movie in which there was a joke about a village idiot. "What if your son was the village idiot?" Those weren't her exact words, but that was what she was saying. It's rough. There are no possible butts of jokes at a certain point in movies. There's almost no one you can make fun of now.

It does seem that we've rid ourselves of many of the taboos surrounding sex and violence, only to replace them with a whole new set. And more are being added everyday.

The women's movement, in particular, has added many taboos. You can't have a dumb blonde any-more, and the dumb blonde was such a wonderful stereotype. There were so many great stereotypes.

Like Franklin Pangborn, the actor from the 1930s and 1940s who always played what used to be called a "pansy."

What a delicious character. I don't know what's wrong with that, although I suppose many people could tell me what's wrong with it. But I think the only thing to do is make jokes about your own failings. I don't know what else I can do about being short.

Under Shawn, *The New Yorker* was famous for its painstaking fact-checking. How did they go about fact-checking your reviews?

Sometimes they made them wrong.

But would the fact-checker go see the movie?

Generally, when I turned in my copy, I would also give them any books or magazines that included data on the references I had made, so they could check them out easily. But in later years, they did go see the movies. In my last year or two writing for the magazine, I was grateful for that, because by that point my Parkinson's was taking a toll on me and I often had a hard time remembering certain things about a movie a few hours later when I sat down to write about it.

You once said that you wanted to write about movies the way that people actually talked about them on leaving the theater.

Yes, the language we really spoke—and the language of movies. I didn't want to write academic English in an attempt to elevate movies, because I think that actually lowers them. It denies them what makes them distinctive.

I remember reading that and thinking, "Wow, Pauline Kael sure has some sophisticated friends," because the people I know tend to say "It was cute" or "It's different" or "It stinks," and let it go at that. But I assume that your first moviegoing companions were your parents and your brothers and sisters.

Yes, it was a big family and I was the youngest, so I saw movies on my parents' laps when I was very young. By the time I was about eight, I started going with other little kids or with my siblings. But, in later years, I would remind them of some of their reactions to the movies we saw, and they didn't remember the movies at all. I was terribly let down by that, because I always assumed that movies had meant as much to them as they did to me. But they hadn't.

Petaluma, California, where you grew up, was farm country in those days?

Chicken-and-egg country, primarily. But it had a couple of movie theaters, and it was close to San Francisco, where our parents would go for music and theater. There was always a lot going on not too far away. As kids, we thought it was a dry, desolate, nothing place. But as you get older you realize it's not a bad little town at all. It was used in *American Graffiti*, and it's been used in a lot of other movies.

Your grandfather worked for Levi Strauss & Company?

That's right.

In what capacity?

He took orders for them. He had traveled around Europe and the Orient. He spoke a number of languages and was a very cultivated man, and he followed his children to California. I was always told that, in Poland, he had worked for a king, buying art objects. And he went to work for Levi Strauss, which in some ways was the equivalent of working for a king.

The king of Northern California.

Yes. I heard nothing but good about Levi Strauss when I was growing up. And I wore practically nothing but jeans.

In those days, the late 1920s and the 1930s, people went to the movies all the time. Did you and your family see pretty much everything that opened?

Everything that came, sure.

And it was usually a double feature?

Unless it was *Ben-Hur*. Often there were two light comedies with actors like Ben Lyon and Bebe

Daniels, and people had a good time—they didn't expect to learn a lesson when they went to the movies. The dialogue was fun in those early talkies. It was delicious—very naughty, and not at all as heavy-handed as dialogue is now.

And if those days were like the 1950s and the 1960s, when I was growing up, young people who were seeing those movies on dates would engage in the same sort of racy banter afterward. When you started dating, were there actors—or actresses, for that matter—that you developed crushes on? And that the boys you dated inevitably failed to measure up to?

I don't think so. For one thing, I tended to like comedy. My favorites were the Ritz Brothers—I'm really crazy about dancer-comedians. They're almost totally forgotten now, though every once in a while Jerry Lewis does a tribute to them, and I suppose that's one way of keeping their names alive, though I wish it were somebody else doing it.

But I loved things that had a faintly surreal comic quality. I never liked Chaplin, because he made me cry, and I didn't want maudlin feelings at the movies. I was very skeptical of Chaplin, because I thought he pushed too hard. In some ways, he did what Spielberg has been doing: He pushes buttons. And because people like that button pushing, they think Spielberg is a great director. But he's become, I think, a very bad director. I thought his Peter Pan movie was just awful. It was closed-in and mean-spirited. And several of his recent movies have really depressed me. *Always* was a shameful movie. Even his best work in *Schindler's List* is very heavy-handed. And I'm a little ashamed for him, because I loved his early work. I loved *The Sugarland Express*. And *1941* was a wonderful comedy. It didn't make it with the public, but he should have had enough brains to know it was a terrific piece of work and to not be so apologetic about it. Instead, he turned to virtuous movies. And he's become so uninteresting now. I think of the work he did in *E.T.* and *Close Encounters*, and I think that he had it in him to become more of a fluid, far-out director. But, instead, he's become a melodramatist.

Did you see *Saving Private Ryan*?

I did. And I was disturbed by the later part, which was so much like the old wartime movies—the sentimental variety. The first part was quite brilliantly effective, but I didn't think it was a good picture. I felt as if Spielberg was bucking for awards, to the point where his people seemed outraged when they didn't win them. As if they deserved honors for their serious intentions.

The invasion of Omaha Beach was good, but why shouldn't it have been? It probably cost as much as the actual invasion. I thought *Saving Private Ryan* and *Schindler's List* were Spielberg's effort to be Oliver Stone—to be weighty and serious and provocative. He's still pulling at the heartstrings, only much more violently than before.

His gift is a much lighter one. What you felt in *E.T.* was a lightness of soul. It's a wonderful gift, and he's working against it. I thought the casting in *Schindler's List* was terribly wrongheaded. The part of Schindler needed a real slickster, a man who got off on fooling the Nazis. Liam Neeson has a lovely voice and a fine presence, but he's just so unexciting—so placid. And if ever a role demanded an actor who showed us that he felt the excitement of the swindle he was pulling, that was it.

Even in the beginning, when he's supposed to be an amoral playboy, you know he's going to turn out decent. I wish the part had been played by Christopher Walken, who's always morally ambiguous.

He's amazing. He has the most extraordinary presence. His dance sequence in *Pennies from Heaven* is one of the joys of our time. And he can be utterly bizarre. Some of the skits he's done hosting *Saturday Night Live*, bumping into things and all, I have to look at him and remember that this is the same man I once saw playing Coriolanus. I remember when I first saw him, in *Next Stop, Greenwich Village*, I didn't know what to make of him.

He played a conceited acting student, and he was so good that you didn't know if he was a conceited actor who could play only that part.

It's such a good movie. Paul Mazursky hasn't been given his due. *Enemies: A Love Story* is one of my favorite movies of all time, and most people haven't even seen it. And *Moon over Parador*, with Richard Dreyfuss as an actor who impersonates a South

American dictator, was quite good. But I'm a sucker for movies about actors, anyway. I love movies in theatrical settings, except for the Jack Benny–Carole Lombard *To Be or Not to Be*. Most of my closest friends are wild about it, but I still don't understand why people find it funny. I've always found it sort of poisonously crude.

You majored in philosophy at Berkeley. Was that with an eye toward teaching?

No. I applied to law school and was accepted. My plan was to teach philosophy while I attended law school, and everyone encouraged me in these plans, but at the last minute I thought, What am I doing, I can't face law school, and I can't face more of the academic life. There are times when you know you've had a bellyful of the academic life. I became involved with a poet and went off and did some writing instead. It was a liberating thing. I think it was good for me. I've regretted it very, very little.

I assume you've received teaching offers over the years, from film departments.

Yes. A number of times, when I've lectured at colleges I've been offered teaching posts. And I was sometimes tempted, because it's a secure living. But I loved writing. I really loved the gamble of writing, the risk-taking. I loved the speed of it, the fact that you had your say and moved on to something else. I'm a very fast person in temperament, and a very fast writer. A weekly was great for me, because by the time something I wrote was printed, I was already working on something else. That was why I couldn't function in Hollywood when I went to work there. Nothing ever seemed over and done with. You would nag over the same material endlessly, discussing the various ramifications and problems, and I hated it.

Early on, you wrote a few radio plays, didn't you?

I wrote a few plays that were done on radio, although they weren't intended for radio and I didn't give my approval. I regretted it when one or two of them appeared on KPFA, in Berkeley.

Could you tell me something about those plays?

I'm not interested in talking about them. I thought then that I had a gift for playwriting, and friends of mine thought so. But I think now that I did not have an imaginative gift. I think I'm ideally suited for criticism, that it satisfies something in me, and that it has the right kinds of creative elements for me. And I really loved doing it.

You published your first piece on movies—on Charlie Chaplin's *Limelight*—in *City Lights* magazine in 1953—

The magazine that Lawrence Ferlinghetti eventually took over, although at that point it was run by Peter Martin, who had started it.

Before you began publishing regularly—and for years afterward—you worked at various other jobs. You ran a repertory cinema, you wrote advertising copy, you worked in a bookstore and as a seamstress and a cook. Some of those were menial jobs, but almost any of them promised a better living than writing, and you had a daughter to support, so what compelled you to—

To write? I don't know. It was insane financially. For years, I was writing for magazines that paid almost nothing, and I was making a few hundred dollars a year by placing pieces in them. Then there was the mild insult of writing for a magazine edited by Amiri Baraka, which paid, as I recall, two dollars per thousand words.

This was *Kulcher*?

That's it. That's what *Kulcher* amounted to—two dollars per thousand words. I wrote for a number of other magazines that paid comparably. I mean, *Partisan Review* was high-paying: I got something like sixty-four dollars for a long article. It was impossible to make a living at the kind of writing I was doing, particularly because I was on the West Coast, and when I got assignments from magazines and papers in New York, they would often reject what I wrote and not pay me any kill fee, because I was across the country and unlikely to bump into them. For a long time, I didn't even know there was such a thing as a kill fee.

Oh, they must have loved you—a real virgin. But at the very beginning of your career, when you

were reviewing movies on the radio in San Francisco—some of the material that was collected in *I Lost It at the Movies*, your first book—you came across as someone intent on undoing damage.

I was often disputing what the New York critics had written, and doing it as a way of alerting people to good movies I thought might pass them by—*The Golden Coach*, *Fires on the Plain*, *The Earrings of Madame de . . .*, *The Innocents*, by Jack Clayton, with Deborah Kerr.

Or occasionally a heavily publicized American movie that the established critics had inexcusably panned, like Stanley Kubrick's *Lolita*.

Lolita in particular. I was trying to do a rescue job, at least for the people in San Francisco, where I was writing and where the movies came a few weeks later. There were tons of marvelous movies that were being ignored because Bosley Crowther, of the *New York Times*, and the other New York critics didn't like them.

It's funny, critics can be as vain as the performers whose vanity they take great pleasure in mock-

ing. As a music critic, I've noticed that anything you say about a performer is okay, no matter how mocking or dismissive. It's when you start taking your colleagues to task in print that you're accused of hitting below the belt. And that was what happened to you.

Yes. I didn't realize the degree to which the New York critics would be angry at this upstart voice from California, because it didn't seem like such a big voice to me. I was doing this on listener-spon-sored radio, and I wasn't being paid. I was doing it because I loved writing and talking about movies. So it was awful to realize the degree of hostility I had built up in New York. And they took it out on me in funny ways.

For example, the idea has spread that I jumped the gun in reviewing *Nashville*. Even Altman says that in interviews now. But there were three large screenings, attended by myself and other critics and held well in advance of opening for the purpose of getting the word out. It was eleven minutes longer than it was when it opened, but it was easy to see what would be cut. Before I wrote about it, I phoned Altman's office and asked one of his representatives if she would check with him to see if he wanted the movie reviewed then or later. She said, "Now—that's why the screenings were held." I loved *Nashville*, and I'm glad that I wrote about it when I did because I think it did it some good. But I was jumped on for being unethical in reviewing the movie early in an attempt to influence opinion. It's become part of film lore, and I suppose there's no way of combating it.

The same thing with *Last Tango in Paris*—they made it appear as if I reviewed that early. I wrote about it after seeing it at the New York Film Festival, where all of the other critics saw it. It was reviewed in quite a few places from that, but most people didn't pay very much attention to it. I did, and I bore the brunt for that. In a way, I shouldn't complain. That review helped to make my name, because it was so roundly attacked. But I felt that I wasn't being given a fair shake.

For years, your nemesis was Andrew Sarris, the other influential movie critic of your generation, who wrote for the *Village Voice*. Your biggest disagreement with him was over the so-called "auteur" theory, which originated in France and

which he more or less imported to the United States.

Well, the auteur theory originally meant something quite different from what people understand it to mean now. What it originally said was that a director conferred value upon a film—that if a director was an auteur, all of his films were great. I think the public never understood that, and neither did most of the press. It was an untenable theory, and it fell from sight. It's now taken to mean that we should pay attention to who directed a movie, because a director is vital to a film, and of course this is true. But it's something that everybody has always known. I mean, everybody knew that Howard Hawks was terrific. We went to see *To Have and Have Not* and *The Big Sleep* the day they opened, and there was an excitement in the theater, because we all knew that these movies were special. They were smart, and we loved the work of smart directors, because lots of movies were so dumb.

But it didn't mean that all of Hawks's movies were great.

No, because he also made a lot of very bad movies, like *Monkey Business*. But the auteurists considered all of his movies to be wonderful by definition, because he was an auteur. It reached a point where they were acclaiming the later movies of directors who had ceased doing good work years earlier. Hitchcock's later movies were acclaimed, and they were stinkers—terrible movies. And many routine action movies were praised because they were the work of certain directors.

But the auteurists would argue that Hawks's methods in a movie like *Monkey Business* revealed something about the approach he took in those other, great movies of his.

But it's sometimes discouraging to see all of a director's movies, because there's so much repetition. The auteurists took this to be a sign of a director's artistry, that you could recognize his movies. But for all of a director's movies to be alike in some essential way can also be a sign that he's a hack.

Yeah, I guess it's a way of seeing falling back on habit as a sign of integrity. Anyway, for all your

differences, I always thought that you and Sarris were alike in many ways. There was a time, not so long ago, when the movie critics for most daily newspapers were also drama critics who made no secret which medium they regarded as superior. There may have been decent movie criticism in literary journals and in some of the slicks, but for the most part it was written by all-around men of letters—Dwight Macdonald, James Agee, Otis Ferguson, Parker Tyler, Robert Warshow, and people like that. You and Sarris were the first dedicated, no-bones-about-it movie critics.

We both loved movies. We had that in common, and I enjoy reading him as I enjoy reading very few critics. He has genuine reactions to movies, and many critics don't. He picks things up and points things out.

There's something else you have in common, too. This isn't going to be an exact quote, but I remember he once wrote that he sometimes didn't know what people were talking about when they described a movie as "erotic," because that was such a subjective question. He said that his only

way of determining if a scene was erotic was if it gave him an erection. That's getting right to the point, and allowing for gender, it sounds like something you might have said.

But the big difference between us is that our taste in movies is so radically different. He really likes romantic, classically structured movies. He had very conservative tastes in movies; he didn't love the far-out stuff that I loved. He's a man who likes movies like *Waterloo Bridge*, movies that drive me crazy with impatience. It's funny that he should have been at the *Voice*, and the voice of an underground paper. I think I would have been much more suitable to *Voice*, yet for years I got dumped on brutally by that paper. That always amazed me, because I thought, I'm praising movies you should love, so what's going on here? He and I were at the wrong places — it's one of those flukes of movie history.

PART TWO

ॐ

Did you ever meet Alfred Hitchcock?

Yes. I was doing preliminary work for a radio show that I had been asked to do, which was never completed, and I taped interviews with him and a number of other people. I didn't have a very good time with him, because he wanted to talk about movies but couldn't, because he hadn't really gone to see anything. His wife had, and she was very knowledgeable and very pleasant. I liked her a lot, but he kept breaking off to talk about his wine cellar and his champagne collection, and these seemed more vital to him than talking about movies.

I got very distressed when we talked about actors, because he had often cast people not after seeing them in pictures but from seeing them on a reel of film that their agents brought him, so that he saw only little highlights from some of their roles. He didn't know the possibilities of some of the actors, and this was reinforced by his feeling that he shouldn't improvise. Directors should not be allowed to improvise, he said, even though he had done a lot of improvisation earlier in his career, and it was some of his best work. I think part of the rigidity of his later pictures was from his feeling that everything should be worked out in advance, which didn't allow for any creative participation by the actors. You feel the absence of that participation in movies like *Topaz* and *Marnie* and—oh, I would say all of his later movies. He was quite rigid, almost like a religious fanatic—no one should improvise, the director should have everything planned out in advance.

Do you think this sometimes resulted in wooden performances, like Sean Connery's in *Marnie*?

Sean Connery I particularly asked about, because I was puzzled why he was so wooden in *Marnie*.

Hitchcock said, "Well, that man never could act, you know, he could only play 007." And I was astonished, because Connery was giving some of his greatest performances—oh, I shouldn't say his greatest performances, because I think he became even better later, when he did *The Man Who Would Be King* and some of his later films. But he was already doing marvelous work in that period, and Hitchcock didn't seem interested in it at all—he didn't seem interested in actors.

When you went to work for Paramount in 1979, at the urging of Warren Beatty, you helped to shepherd some movies into production, right?

Yeah, but I'd rather not talk about that, because in some cases the directors didn't know I had a hand in getting their movies produced.

It was reported at the time that your first assignment was a project directed by James Toback.

Yes, but I decided very early on that I didn't want to do that. Warren was very understanding, and I was made a general consultant, rather than specifically tied to the Toback project.

In contrast to Hitchcock, do you think Toback takes the idea of improvisation a little too far?

I think Toback is immensely gifted, but I don't see that he's developing as a director. He has energy and ideas, but I think he takes it too far in terms of not working out the script, letting the actors say what they want to say and develop their characters. I loved the kind of improvisation Altman did in things like *Nashville*, where he blended the actors' experiences with the characters'. Toback isn't that gifted and he isn't that patient. He tends to take all kinds of risks, and then he tries to put the picture together in the editing room. And I don't think the results have been interesting enough.

It's funny. Often, when people talk about improvisation in movies, they make a comparison with jazz. What they don't realize is that jazz improvisation isn't quite as unfettered as they think.

Yes, and if you listen to several performances by the same musician, it's amazing how similar his improvisations are. When I spoke at colleges, I liked to improvise and to talk directly to the audiences. I used a prepared text no more than once or twice over the many years. But when I would hear a tape of one of my talks on the radio, often I would think, Well, that's almost exactly what I said last week. You tend, when you improvise, to go back to the same themes. You talk around the same subjects, and it's often not as fresh as you imagine it is.

We were talking earlier about Jean-Luc Godard, whose early movies you championed.

I haven't seen many of his more recent ones, because I haven't been in New York for the last decade. I feel very cut off from what he's doing anyway. I don't feel drawn to it at all. I think that for a while he was perhaps the most important French director since [Jean] Renoir. He did absolutely stunning new work. He did what Altman was doing in this country—they were rather parallel in their thinking, in using the journalistic form and making films that were like essays. He was an amazing director, and maybe what he's doing now is still amazing, but I haven't seen the movies. I've seen a few of them, and I didn't feel the excitement that I felt when I saw *Band of Outsiders* or *La Chinoise* or any one of a dozen of his earlier movies. There are amazing sequences in his *Les Carabiniers*. It's not a very interesting movie, but sometimes we'll settle for a brilliant image or sequence or performance. A lot of W.C. Fields comedies I love for a particular sequence, and the rest of it doesn't matter very much. I think that's true of a lot of movies that count with us.

I assume you eventually met Godard. What was he like?

I spent social afternoons with him early in his career, and he was very amiable. His English wasn't great, but it was good enough to communicate, and there would be other people around who would sometimes help with a word or two. We had a good time talking about movies. This was after his first few movies, before he became difficult. Later, he became quite hostile, and I don't know if this was because his more political films didn't please me in the same way that his earlier films had. The enthusiasm I'd felt for films like *Band of Outsiders* and *Masculine-Feminine* and *La Chinoise* and *Weekend*, I didn't feel for his next films, and he may have been reacting to that.

It's always painful to get to know a director, because they almost always take it very personally when you don't like a film. No matter how much you loved their other work, a negative review takes precedence in their thinking.

Were there directors, though, who would just let criticism bounce off them?

They didn't let it bounce off them, but some of them were gracious about it. John Boorman was incredibly kind. I felt absolute misery on one occasion when I'd seen a film of his and then we met for drinks and I tried to avoid the subject of the film, and he told me years later that he understood my agony. Some performers have been kind, and some have been extremely kind. Barbra Streisand was incredibly pleasant when I gave her a very rough review in *Funny Lady*. She phoned to make me feel better, which is unusual for an actor to do. Generally, they become really hostile about almost anything negative you say. I mean, one line in a

review that's otherwise positive and they never for-
give you.

**One last question about Godard. I've recently
watched many of his early movies again, and
many of François Truffaut's. When I first saw
those movies, in the late 1960s, I was in my early
twenties and partial to Godard, because Truffaut
seemed so middle-class and traditional, whereas
Godard was as much a revolutionary politically
as he was aesthetically.**

I think the movies that Truffaut made after *The Wild
Child* and [*The Story of*] *Adele H.* were like the movies
he'd panned as a critic, for representing "the tradition of quality."* Some of those movies he disliked
were actually a lot better than the later ones he
made.

---

*In "Une Certaine Tendance du Cinéma Français," published in
Cahiers du Cinéma in 1954, Truffaut attacked that era's French cinema
for adhering to a distanced "tradition of quality," and called for a
more personal approach to filmmaking. The essay was both a cor-
nerstone of auteur theory and the first manifesto of the French *nou-
velle vague.*

It surprises me, though, that early Truffaut still seems fresh and holds up so much better than early Godard. I still think of Godard's early movies as great movies. But with the possible exception of *Breathless*, they didn't really hold up. You'd think the idea that a thing of beauty is a joy forever would be as true of movies as it is of other art forms.

I don't think it is true. I think movies are a popular art form, and they can mean a great deal to us at the time—mean something new—but they get stale very quickly, as what they do is imitated. Also, you can't underestimate Godard's journalistic side. He was commenting on his time—"the children of Marx and Coca Cola."* *Breathless* might hold up better than some of the others, but all of his movies were like very quick skits. Altman's films may hold up better, too—the big ones. I think Altman has made a fantastic number of great movies, or very good ones. But his aren't journalistic, finally. They're like watching several TV stations at once. I don't know how to account for the fact that when

---

*A line from *Masculine-Feminine*.

he's good, he's superb, and when he isn't good, he's nothing. I can't accept the films he's just tossed off.

Did you like *Cookie's Fortune*?

I thought it was quite good. It's not in a class with *Thieves Like Us*, *Nashville*, *McCabe and Mrs. Miller*, *The Long Goodbye*, and *California Split*. But it's a charming, fragrant movie with a beautiful structure. The way it all turns out to be about a family is lovely, because you don't anticipate that. And it's fun to see Patricia Neal come through with a fine performance.

You were famous—infamous some might say— for never seeing a movie more than once.

That's right.

But now that you have—

More time? I still don't look at movies twice. It's funny, I just feel I got it the first time. With music it's different, although I realize that sometimes with classical works, I listen to them with great enthusiasm and excitement the first time, but I'm not drawn to listen to them again and again. Whereas with pop, it's just the reverse. Give me Aretha singing "A Rose Is Just a Rose," and I can play it all day long. And I can't explain that.

Do you think that seeing even a movie you love no more than once is, in some ways, characteristic of your generation? I mean, in the days before repertory houses and cable movie channels and video cassettes, a new movie came to your neighborhood, you saw it, and then it was gone. You remembered the good ones, but you were rarely given an opportunity to see them again.

Well, often when you were a kid, you would stay for the next show, so you saw the movie again that same day. But you don't do that when you grow up. At least I don't.

As a matter of fact, they no longer let you stay for another show.

Yes, they clear the house now and try to make it seem that it's for your benefit.

They say they have to sweep.

Only they don't sweep. But I can't explain some of these things—why people respond so differently to the whole issue of seeing a movie many times. I'm astonished when I talk to really good critics, who know their stuff and will see a film eight or ten or twelve times. I don't see how they can do it without hating the movie. I would.

So you haven't broken down and decided, I'm going to watch *Nashville* again today?

No. I was thinking about it, because this new— what are the initials?

DVD?

—is supposed to be coming out, and because I just read an absolutely splendid article on *Nashville* that was downloaded for me from *Salon*. It's by Ray Sawhill, and I think it's the best piece on movies I've read all year. It recalled for me the excitement I felt when I wrote about *Nashville*, twenty-five years ago.

It's fun reading terrific articles and reviews. There just aren't enough of them. Most of the good people now seem to be on the Web, writing for *Salon* or *Slate*.

Do you cruise the Web for reviews?

I don't cruise anything. They get downloaded for me by friends. I'm a mechanical idiot and always have been. That's why I wrote by hand. It became sort of an organic process, but I think it was an excuse so I wouldn't have to learn to operate the machinery.

Beginning with the typewriter?

That's right. I've never typed. I always wrote in pencil, and very fast.

As a point of curiosity, did you hand your copy in at *The New Yorker* in longhand?

Sometimes. But most of the time, my daughter or someone else would type it up for me. Sometimes I would have it typed up and then redo it, so it would be half-longhand. It didn't make a hell of a lot of difference to the printers as long as you wrote legibly.

I hear that you've been watching a lot of TV.

I watch a few programs regularly, and people seem surprised by that, so they think I watch a lot more than I do. *The West Wing* and, let's see, *Sex and the City*, but there's not much else. They're more interesting than most of the movies I've seen lately.

I'm surprised that you didn't mention *The Sopranos*.

I would have talked very enthusiastically about it if you'd asked me a year ago. I loved the first season and watched it religiously. I thought there was marvelous stuff in it, especially from Nancy Marchand as the mother. She was such a surprise in that role. But it seems to have gotten rather crude and routine. It gets talked about more than it deserves.

Most TV series wear thin so fast. If you don't catch them when they're hot, they're never that good again.

Do you think that's because they have to keep bringing back the same characters week after week?

The same characters, and basically the same situation gets repeated. And my interest usually doesn't extend past the tenth episode or so.

How did even that first season of *The Sopranos* stack up against the first two *Godfather* movies or *GoodFellas*?

It stacked up well against *GoodFellas*, which I thought was pretty weak. But *The Godfather*—that's like comparing each new movie to Eisenstein. The first two *Godfather* movies are perhaps the best movies ever made in this country. It's unfair to ask a TV series to live up to that. But *The Sopranos* had a quality of its own. It had its own humor. The leading man had such a wonderfully vulgar charm. I mean, if there was ever a character who stood for the common man, it was him. Watching the rise and fall of his gut was enough to keep you amused from week to week.

How does *The West Wing* compare to something like *Primary Colors*, which I understand you liked?

It stacks up pretty well, even though there have been some pretty weak episodes. The stuff with the president's daughter and the black aide was perhaps a bit too noble. But it's a good show. It's got more going for it than any other program I know of on TV at the moment—except maybe for the animation shows, but I don't have the stomach for animation. The casting is so good. The women are beautiful, and they're actresses who generally don't get good roles. It's fun to see Stockard Channing as the First Lady. I only wish she were in it more.

Do you think Martin Sheen makes a credible president?

He's as credible as most presidents in the media. He's not bad. He's such a noble, decent weakling that it's rather touching. And the men in the back rooms of the White House are such perfect types. They look like men who could be in an administration. They're very convincing and very funny.

Primary Colors is really a very entertaining movie, and I hadn't been led to think so from the reviews. Most people I know didn't go to see it. I was surprised to find that it had perhaps Mike Nichols's best work in it. He's not a director I'm ordinarily very enthusiastic about, and it had an unfortunate script, but Nichols brought style and pacing to it, and God knows we can use some style and pacing in movies now.

John Travolta is an actor who has so much truth and earnestness in him that you sometimes don't know whether to take him straight. But he's a wonderful actor. His performance as Clinton in *Primary Colors* was a joyous performance, and a difficult one—it wasn't just a matter of impersonation. But I've also seen him in dumb movies where I couldn't believe that he approached the material with such sincerity. I can't think of anyone else like that, who's has that quality of sincerity. He's a remarkable actor. He plays simpletons and does it with such heartfelt feeling that he carries you right along. But I've noticed that when he appears on TV talk shows, there's a tendency for the hosts to patronize him a little bit, because the assumption is he's not a very smart guy. But whether he's smart or not, he's a remarkable actor.

Do you think his being a Scientologist has something to do with the way he's treated?

Probably, but they don't patronize Tom Cruise. Tom Cruise gets by with it much better, although he doesn't get by much better with his acting.

Well, Tom Cruise doesn't have Vinnie Barbarino to live down.

That's true. Tom Cruise never played working-class boys. He was always a very middle-class boy.

I understand that you were also impressed with Mike Nichols as an actor in the film version of Wallace Shawn's play *The Designated Mourner*.

Oh, I am—inordinately impressed. I can't believe anyone could bring off that performance the way he did. He plays a sleazebag, and plays it just superlatively. It's a very strange play. I don't know how to react to it at times. I've tried to lure friends into watching it, but I don't think any of them has made it all the way through. So it may be a fluke that I really love it. I've looked at it three or four times, and I almost never look at a movie even twice. It's a bewildering, fascinating movie.

Maybe what turns people off is that it's a series of monologues, with Nichols and the other characters speaking directly to the camera.

I liked *My Dinner with Andre* more than most people did, too. I really thought that was wonderful. It had more to say about the theater, about lives in the theater, than practically any other movie I've ever seen.

***My Dinner with Andre* at least gained a cult following. The funny thing, though, was that most people who saw it identified with Andre Gregory—**

Not I.

Rather than with Wallace Shawn, who was the soul of the movie.

I couldn't identify with Andre Gregory, because he represents a sort of rich dilettante's point of view. The willingness of that character to go for every mystic cult that came down the pike made it difficult to take him seriously. On the other hand, Wally Shawn, playing the common man, also went a little too far with it. But it's great fun, a wonderful movie.

Let's talk about *Sex and the City*.

Sex and the City is terrific. It's held my interest longer because it's only a half hour, and because those girls are so spectacularly funny. They really are amazing. It feels new, because in the past they wouldn't have dared to put material like that on television—those girls discussing men the way that men discuss women, and going pretty far. There are episodes that really break me up, that I can't get out of my mind. Like the episode where Kim Cattrall goes to bed with a very rich older man who explains to her that he knows he's old and not very appealing to a young woman, but that he will take good care of her. He gives her jewelry. They go to bed together, and when he excuses himself to go the bathroom, she gets a look at his naked rear end and flees the apartment. The truth of the matter is that she's a gold digger, but she's not that *much* of a gold digger. It's hysterically funny, and she's awfully good.

Do you think that television now routinely pulls things off that movies, for whatever reason, no longer seem able to do?

Well, no, because movies have already done those things and can't keep doing them over and over. That's why I have no interest in seeing the big epics, like *Gladiator*. They redo the epic movies I grew up with, like *Ben-Hur*, and I don't want to see them again. *Sex and the City* is like an old movie with Joan Blondell as a gold digger, called *Three Broadway Girls*. It was also shown as *The Greeks Had a Word for Them*. The same basic material turns up. You can't make a movie out of it anymore, but you can make a very good half-hour television show.

I should have included *Frasier* on the list of things I watch on TV, except there are so many repeats that you never know if it's going to be one you've already seen. But David Hyde Pierce is terrific as the brother, and the shows are very cleverly structured. Sitcoms can be tiresome. You don't want to see an episode a second time. At least with *Frasier*, if you catch it again and there's nothing else to watch, you can tolerate it. I was never as fond of *Seinfeld* as I am of *Frasier*, though I wish they'd give John Mahoney better material. He's been doing the same routine as the father for a long time.

He's good, too. I liked him in Costa-Gavras's *Betrayed*, with Debra Winger, though I disliked the movie.

Debra Winger — lord, she was good. Did you ever see *Mike's Murder*? She was sensational in that, and in so many other movies. She was wonderful opposite Travolta in *Urban Cowboy*; they played together beautifully. I don't know whether her retirement from the screen was voluntary, or if nobody was offering her good roles. There aren't that many good roles being offered to any of the women around now. And Meg Ryan turns up in every movie you don't want to go to see.

It bothered me in the early nineties, though, when every paper and magazine seemed to be running a think piece about why there were so

few good women's roles and so few good movies
for women to see—

There were none for men, either.

**Right. But this was around the time of *Six Degrees
of Separation*, with that transcendent performance by Stockard Channing, and *Household
Saints*, with fine roles for Tracey Ullman and Lili
Taylor—underpublicized movies that the critics
who wrote those articles should have been urging
both men and women to see, but didn't seem to
know about. Around the same time, there was a
nice little movie called *Imaginary Crimes* that
almost no one saw, with a striking performance
by the young actress Fairuza Balk.**

Oh, she is wonderful, isn't she?

**But she's hardly in anything. She was in that
movie with Edward Norton, *American History X*,
but she was wasted in that.**

She's one of the best actresses in movies, and she's
been in them since she was a child. Yet somehow,

she never gets the buildup. She and Amanda Plummer, whom I'm crazy about, play sisters in a movie that hasn't opened, called *Blue Murder*, and they're wonderful together. Amanda Plummer is one of God's gifts to the screen, and directors don't seem to know it.

She's hardly in anything, either, although Tarantino used her in *Pulp Fiction*.

By the way, I loved what Tarantino did with Bridget Fonda and Robert De Niro in that one sequence in *Jackie Brown* where she keeps goading him and goading him until he pulls out his gun and shoots her dead. It's so surprising, it's perfect. It's a wonderful sequence. I liked that movie.

Do you think one virtue of television is its more lenient casting? I'm thinking of actors like Travolta, Bruce Willis, Michael J. Fox, Jim Carrey, Tom Hanks—movie stars who first got noticed on television and who, without television, might never have been thought to have what it takes to be leading men in movies.

Well, that was true of earlier generations of stars as well. In their first appearances, they often played gangsters or hoods, someone uncouth. Clark Gable, at first, was a villain—an uncouth bastard. *Night Nurse*, with Barbara Stanwyck. He was a tough customer in that.

Men are more interesting in romantic roles when you've already seen them playing tough guys. Tom Hanks didn't come up that route, but he played some oddball characters. He was wonderful on television in *Bosom Buddies*. He's much less interesting now, I think.

Is there anyone you see on television now who you think has untapped movie potential?

Can you think of anyone? I can't, offhand. There are people who I enjoy, and who surprise me. I like Cynthia Nixon a lot. She's the tall redhead in *Sex and the City*. I've seen her give wonderful performances on stage. And then she turned up on *Law & Order*, I think. That show often has good people, because it's shot in New York and they avail themselves of people from Broadway theater. I think that's one of the reasons that show has sustained itself over the years. When I watch it, I'm astonished by how they can use the same format week after week, and yet the performances hold you. The actors might be people you've never seen before, but you discover that they're respected figures in New York theater.

Do you periodically watch MTV or VH–1 to catch up with what's happening in pop music?

I should but I don't, because I don't have to keep up with it anymore. MTV just doesn't interest me very much. What being cut off from movies has done, I'm afraid—I know it's not supposed to have this effect, but I read with greater intensity. Friends used to make fun of the fact that I would read and watch TV simultaneously, because they assumed that the book would almost always take over. But I was able to do those two things at once. Now I find if I'm reading something of interest, the TV can't compete.

Do you find yourself becoming alienated from popular culture?

No, because I love the energy of pop, which I miss in classical music. I find I tend to buy more pop than classical music, which rather alarms me, because my early education was in the classics. But pop has a bite to it—a life to it. And I think that one of the reasons we love movies so much is that they have that pop element. It's why so many plays seem deadly to audiences today. They have such a refined texture to them, and they put you to sleep with all that refinement.

What have you been listening to lately?

I'm crazy about Tom Waits, which puzzles me, because the first time I heard him—on the sound-track of an Altman movie, I think—I was rather hostile to it. It seemed blurry and noisy to me. But for the last year or so, I've been really wild about him. I love his lyrics. I've got *The Mule Variations*, *Rain Dogs*, *Frank's Wild Years*, and a few others. And, of course, you can play CDs and read at the same time without any conflict, although in his case, I tend to stop reading and concentrate on the music. It's always interesting to see what wins out in the battle of the arts.

I've gotten interested in some things I never really liked. I was never as crazy about Duke Ellington as you're supposed to be, but then just this week Howard Hampton, the music critic, sent me Ellington's *Such Suite Thunder*, and I flipped over it. I must have played it ten or fifteen times already. Howard also recently sent me Martial Solal's *Just Friends*.* He has great taste. I don't think he's ever sent me anything I didn't love.

I've always been a freak for Sister Rosetta Tharpe.† I love her, but I never saw her perform. Someone apparently heard that I loved her and sent me a video, seventeen minutes that he put together of her from various sources. I just loved seeing her singing gospel and playing guitar so incredibly fast. I've rarely gotten a present from someone I didn't know that went to my heart so completely. It's a wonderful piece of film.

Let's talk a little more about TV. I'm curious to know what you made of all the fanfare surround-

---

*Solal is a French jazz pianist who composed the score for Godard's *Breathless*.

†An American gospel singer and guitarist who was at the peak of her popularity in the early 1940s, when she performed with Lucky Millander's big band.

ing Michael J. Fox's departure from *Spin City* a few months ago, after he revealed that he had Parkinson's.

The only thing that bothered me was that it was a terrible episode. They publicized it so heavily, and I was hoping that it would be a good show, because a lot of people who don't know Michael J. Fox's work in movies watched it, and they really would have no idea of how talented he was and what good work he's done over the years. The show didn't do him justice, and I felt bad about that.

Did it also bother you for a more personal reason?

Because of my own Parkinson's? No, because even though I could sense that his body movement was being dictated by the Parkinson's, I could see that he worked that into the role. I feel more upset when I see Janet Reno, because she's in a terrible, vulnerable position, and the press has been so unkind to her—the Parkinson's just seems like an extra blow. The press can be extraordinarily cruel, and I've heard remarks made about her on television talk shows that I can't believe I'm hearing—that people can be that grossly insensitive. But she's a remarkable woman, and there's something very gutsy about the fact that she hasn't tried to conceal the symptoms. She could hide her hands under a desk or something, but she hasn't.

In Fox's case, I wish that instead of inventing a political scandal for his character on *Spin City*, the script had acknowledged his Parkinson's as the reason for the character leaving his job.

That would have been sensible, wouldn't it, since everyone knew. I don't know why they did it that way. There were probably big backstage arguments about it. It was unfortunate, a very sloppy show.

The week the episode aired, you were featured in a sidebar to a *Newsweek* cover story on Fox and Parkinson's. A mutual friend of ours told me that you complained that they had left out the humorous things you had to say about being afflicted.

Well, I'm somewhat more chipper about it than most people. I think I was a little unfair to them — they would have had to bring in some jokes I made about the disease, which wasn't what they were after. People want to take these things lugubriously, and they want you to be a victim. I had Parkinson's my last ten years at the magazine, and it affects recent memory very radically, so I often found myself phoning friends or the checkers and asking them what happened in a certain scene, or where the scene took place. I'd lost confidence in my memory. But I don't feel like a victim. I've been very, very lucky, and I've handled the medication well. And as maddening as it can be—I mean, here I am with my legs writhing, but I don't feel as bad about the Parkinson's as I did a few years ago. I've learned to control it somewhat. The trouble is, you use up your years on the medication, and you know that the side effects are going to take over hideously.

I assume that your Parkinson's was the reason you retired from *The New Yorker*.

That plus the fact that I suddenly couldn't say anything about some of the movies. They were just so terrible, and I'd already written about so many terrible movies. I love writing about movies when I can discover something in them—when I can get something out of them that I can share with people. The week I quit, I hadn't planned on it. But I wrote up a couple of movies, and I read what I'd written, and it was just incredibly depressing. I thought, I've got nothing to share from this.

One of them was of that movie with Woody Allen and Bette Midler, *Scenes from a Mall*. I couldn't write another bad review of Bette Midler. I thought she was so brilliant, and when I saw her in that terrible production of *Gypsy* on television, my heart sank. And I'd already panned her in *Beaches*. How can you go on panning people in picture after picture when you know they were great just a few years before? You have so much emotional investment in praising people that when you have to pan the same people a few years later, it tears your spirits apart.

Yet, that's not the way that people imagine that critics operate. They imagine that critics love sitting there and coming up with witty put-downs.

Oh, no. It's awful, particularly if you loved an actor's earlier work. And Woody Allen didn't deserve to be as bad as he was in *Scenes from a Mall*, either. I don't feel great enthusiasm about his recent movies, but I thought parts of *Husbands and Wives* were quite stunning. I loved Judy Davis in it. I think she's perhaps the best woman working in movies since Debra Winger took off. She gives performances like nothing I've ever seen before, and she was stunning opposite Sydney Pollack in *Husbands and Wives*. But nothing of Woody Allen's that I've seen since has really excited me.

It really is depressing. You can't explain some of these things, except that it's the wrong material, the wrong costars, everything goes wrong in a movie when something goes wrong, and it's just too damn depressing to spend your life writing about that.

You've often surprised interviewers by telling them that your favorite decade for movies was the 1970s. They expect you to say the 1930s or the 1940s, a period long enough ago to seem classic.

I love the fact that I wrote about movies in the seventies, when there were directors coming along who really brought something new to the medium. Just think, I got to write about Godard and Truffaut, and Altman and Coppola, and movies that people don't even talk about, like Hal Ashby's *The Landlord*, which was a wonderful movie from the 1970s.

Yet when you returned to *The New Yorker* in 1980, after your sojourn in Hollywood working for Warren Beatty, your first piece was an essay called "Why Are Movies So Bad? or, The Numbers." It happened that quickly—the stakes became too high to allow for the same sort of experimentation?

That's exactly what happened. A few movies made inordinate amounts of money, and everything we hoped for from movies went kerplooie. A good movie brought in terrible consequences. *Jaws* is really a terrific movie. I laughed all the way through it. Yet it marked something. Then, with *Star Wars* coming on top of it—that awful *Star Wars* and its successors—movies have just never been the same. The direction in which we thought they were moving, they've gone the other way.

There are hardly any small movies that people go to, and some of the more interesting ones they

won't go to. I loved *Three Kings*, which I thought
was probably the best American movie I saw last
year. But it didn't have much of a following, even
with George Clooney in the lead, and he was very
good. Larry Kasdan's *Mumford*, which was dismissed in the press, I thought was a charming
movie. It was witty and charming and light. But for
some strange reason we don't go to charming, light
movies anymore. People expect a movie to be
heavy and turgid, like *American Beauty*. They want
movies to be about our misery and alienation and
what rotters we all are. So if you make a lighthearted movie about a small town, nobody goes. It's
very difficult, I think, for a critic to persuade people to see a lighthearted movie. We've become a
heavy-handed society.

**It's as though we want movies to be good for us,
to be medicinal in some way—**

Yes, isn't that awful?

**Instead of just being pleasurable. Along with the
financial stakes becoming higher, did something
else begin to go wrong with movies in the late**

1970s? Did a certain political correctness begin to creep in, starting around the time of *Coming Home*?

Coming Home depressed me, because people took it so seriously. Jane Fonda was so virtuous, and Jon Voight was such a good guy. I mean, there's something depressing about your liberal friends falling for a movie in which the liberal is a paraplegic and a great lover, and the soldier is a villain and a lousy lover. The movies have gone on from there. *American Beauty* has the same sort of stuff. It's hard to believe that people who, in the sixties and early seventies, seemed to be opening their minds a little bit would close them down again in the name of political correctness.

It's the cinema of good intentions.

Yes, the cinema of good intentions.

Not being able to write about movies now must be frustrating, because there's a lot of damage that needs undoing at this point.

I keep seeing movies I think are interesting that nobody is praising. *Three Kings*, in particular, got some good reviews, but nothing like it deserved. I thought *Mission to Mars* had some extraordinary sequences in it. I'm always attacked for liking Brian De Palma so much, and it's a very uneven, erratic movie. But about half of it is superb, and I can't understand why more people didn't recognize that.

People did latch on to *The Matrix*. I would find it very hard to explain why I liked it so much, but I think it's awfully good. There are movies that are really entertaining, and I don't know why they're so entertaining. *Magnolia* was one of them. I had an awfully good time at it, and I can't explain why. I mean, I'd have to sit down and really think about it, and I don't know that it bears all that much thought. There are a number of movies that I've liked for rather strange reasons. There was one that had very good fast cutting—*High Fidelity*. The ends of the scenes seemed lopped off in a way that really worked, that gave it a little pulse and added up to a style. *High Fidelity* isn't a bad little movie. It gets better as it goes along. By the end of it, I really was having a good time.

Let's see, what else? Oh, I liked *Flirting with Disaster*, the movie that David O. Russell made before *Three Kings*. I think it's the best simple comedy from this country that I've seen in recent years. Lily Tomlin, Alan Alda, Mary Tyler Moore, and the other people in it are really very funny. There haven't been many recent simple comedies like that, and maybe we've gotten out of the habit of praising them as much as they deserve.

I love movies that are more exploratory. I loved a French movie from a few years ago that very few people saw, a Bertrand Blier film called *My Man*, which got almost no press, but had something of the qualities of *Last Tango*. There aren't very many movies that get at something new. There were scenes in *The Conformist* that movies hadn't approached before, and Bertolucci did another good movie a couple of years ago called *Besieged*, starring Thandie Newton, who's also in *Mission Impossible II*. She's extraordinarily sensitive and interesting, but the film never took off and the press didn't talk about it very much. It's very hard to get people to go see movies that aren't as well publicized as *The Perfect Storm* or *The Patriot*. I can't believe people I know go to see those movies. What do they get out of them?

Well, now that people see fewer movies, might they have a greater investment in liking the few that they do see? Especially if they've been told a movie is likely to be nominated for Oscars and their local critic has given it three-and-a-half stars.

I think it's the publicity that gets to them, although they do take their local critics quite seriously and their local critics pan some of the more interesting movies, because they're oddball and unusual. You find very few local critics who will urge you to see *Besieged*.

It does seem to me that there's a pack mentality among movie critics now, which is ironic in that you were often accused of forcing your opinions on a group of younger critics that your detractors referred to as "Paulettes." As an aside, I should tell you about a story that was making the rounds when *Schindler's List* came out in 1993. I heard from a number of people that one of the reasons

it was getting such unanimously adoring reviews was that you had seen it early and given it your blessing. But I happened to be talking with you on the phone one day a few weeks after it came out, and you told me you hadn't even seen it yet — it hadn't come to your local multiplex, and Spielberg hadn't sent it to you. But there does seem to be what amounts to a party line on most movies now, with the reviewers taking their cues from the studios and the festival organizers, and then sucking up to one another. Nobody wants to be the odd man out and say, Wait a minute, this supposedly prestigious movie stinks. Or this movie that the studio has lost faith in is really worth seeing.

I think you're right to some degree. There are some good critics at the moment. David Edelstein, of *Slate*, is absolutely first-rate. And Elvis Mitchell, of the *Times*, has a real feeling for pop and a real energy in his approach to it. There are several good people at *Salon*. Stephanie Zacharek is very good and so is her husband, Charles Taylor. And I think Ray Sawhill does the best think pieces of anyone around.

But there is a pack mentality. It affects the small-town critics more than the individuals who write for *Salon* or *Slate*. I sometimes read these really very well-educated men writing their hearts out on crap, and I'm depressed because they're wasting so much first-rate intellect on such low-grade material. That's one of the reasons I quit. I just felt I couldn't go on doing that.

Do you think that many of today's younger critics are careerists in a way that you never were and someone like Andrew Sarris never was? They don't necessarily want to spend the rest of their lives writing film criticism. They envision being asked to write scripts, and they can't afford to write anything that might alienate someone in a position to give them a break at some point in the future.

It's happened in a few cases, but it hasn't been very successful. They haven't gotten anywhere, except for payoffs on a few bum scripts. But I don't think that's what's the matter. I think it's more complicated than that. It's difficult to be a critic of mass culture. You write about so much crap that you begin to be contemptuous of what you're writing about — at least, a lot of critics are, and they hope for something more interesting to do. You can't fault them for that. But they don't do justice to what they're seeing. They don't seem to be sensitive to what's on the screen. I don't know how so many people could have panned so many brilliant movies. I mean, the best movies of our time have been panned, and there doesn't seem to be any excuse for it — the critics have had training in film, they've gone to very good colleges, and they don't seem able to spontaneously recognize quality.

When you say that, two movies I immediately think of are Brian De Palma's *Casualties of War*, and *Pennies from Heaven*, with Steve Martin and Bernadette Peters, both of which you were practically alone in reviewing enthusiastically.

I can't believe those movies didn't get more press support. It seems inconceivable that people could work in a medium and not see the qualities in *Casualties of War*. Sean Penn gives one of his finest performances in it, Michael J. Fox is amazingly good, and they play off each other beautifully. De

Palma uses the foxholes as if they were an ant colony: We see everything that's going on in a large area, and then it narrows down to the horror of what the soldiers do to one particular girl. I've never seen a war movie that was as beautifully felt, with the exception of a classic like *Grand Illusion*. It's a little shaky at the end, where it's cut too much. It needed to be longer, but it's really a great movie. You feel it when you see it: You know this is something new, that it's saying something new.

The same thing is true of *Pennies from Heaven*. I mean, Bernadette Peters just goes to your soul. The sequence in the school room, where the fat boy is humiliated by the principal just tears you apart, because you've just seen him so happy.

It was a heartbreaking movie, and the odd thing about watching it was that I found myself moved almost to tears during the musical numbers — the happy scenes.

Dennis Potter always said he wanted his material done in M-G-M musical style, and finally it was, and the movie was attacked because it wasn't like the television version, which didn't have anything

like the dramatic staging or the dynamic performances of an M-G-M musical. It's heartbreaking
when something really gets done right and doesn't
get support. It's difficult to get an audience to go see
a musical anyway, and you really need enormous
press support for something that's difficult and com-
plex, and *Pennies from Heaven* didn't get it. You begin
to despair when people do their finest work and
don't get credit for it.

PART THREE

ॐ

A while ago, you mentioned Jacques Demy's *Bay of Angels*, which I first saw dubbed into English on television years ago, but which I might not have known to keep an eye out for if not for your capsule on it in *Kiss Kiss Bang Bang*. For a lot of us, that section at the end of that book, with the short notices, was a kind of bible. It alerted me to so many good movies I might otherwise never have seen—*Outcasts of the Islands*, for example, which is one of the most haunting movies ever made.

A wonderful movie. Carol Reed made so many wonderful movies. He hasn't had his due.

Let me ask you about a few fairly recent movies. Have you seen the remake of *Lolita*?

I saw it, and it depressed the hell out of me. I really love the Kubrick version. I still think it's one of the funniest things I've ever seen, and I don't know what the hell was going on in the remake, but they took the material seriously in all the wrong ways and they lost the humor that made the original so extraordinary. You know, for some of us, Shelley Winters's performance and James Mason's scenes in the bathtub are among the great treasures of moviegoing. And Peter Sellers was brutally funny. I don't think he was ever better.

What did you make of Kubrick's *Eyes Wide Shut*?

It was ludicrous from the word go.

It was, wasn't it? And you know, something I think that nobody has pointed out is that Tom Cruise is supposed to be a GP—we see him treating small children and the elderly—but he lives in a manner that few top specialists could afford, and in midtown Manhattan no less.

Remember *Play It Again, Sam*? Woody Allen plays a critic for *Film Quarterly*, and he lives very well off that. I wrote for *Film Quarterly*, and they paid somewhere between twenty-five and forty dollars for a long article! And in *Shoot the Moon*, which was made by Alan Parker, a woman is having a tennis court built for $12,000, and that's supposed to be a bargain. I mean, I come from that part of the country, and a bargain would be maybe $2,000. The people who put these movies together have lived high for so long they have no sense of reality anymore.

I think the only scene that anyone's going to remember from *Eyes Wide Shut* years from now is the one where Cruise and Nicole Kidman are making love in front of a mirror, and we hear Chris Isaak singing "They Did a Bad, Bad Thing"—

Yes, the music was fun.

But they're married, so how exactly are they doing a bad, bad thing by making love? Is Kubrick telling us that sex is dirty, even for married couples?

Well, that orgy was the most hygienic thing I've ever seen. It was strangely decorous. What was that all about, and who were these people that they had the money to stage such things?

People who have $12,000 to spend on a tennis court, I guess.

It really is a creepily bad movie. I don't understand why people were so willing to give Kubrick the benefit of the doubt when a lot of talented directors don't get the benefit of the doubt. Jonathan Demme, for example, has—not a large talent, but a charming talent, and he's done movies that haven't gotten any support at all. He has a real knack for using popular music and bringing it right into the movie. He does things with music that I don't think anybody else has done—putting the singers in the side of the frame, in some cases, so you get a duplication of effect—and he makes it work. And then he got vast support for *The Silence of the Lambs*, which was a hideous and obvious piece of moviemaking. I guess it was subtle by the standards of its genre, but it's a nothing piece of work compared to movies he'd made in the past, like *Melvin and Howard* and *Citizen's Band* and *Something Wild*.

I don't know why it is that people who truly love movies, as most critics do, are often so blind to what's on the screen. There are movies that aren't great, but that really are fun, like *Snake Eyes*, the De Palma film. Everything in that movie is done within one large set, in a way that's really amazing. Why didn't that movie get appropriate notice? And people get acclaim for tedious little *film noir* things that are so dull and that go on endlessly. There's nothing going on in most of those movies, and they get the best press in the world.

Have you seen Jim Jarmusch's *Ghost Dog*, with Forest Whitaker?

No. I haven't been fond of Jim Jarmusch's movies. But I love Forest Whitaker. I think he's one of our best actors. I thought he was the one who deserved an award for *The Crying Game*. It was he who did something of great distinction in it. His death scene was amazing.

But that scene occurred early in the movie, and audiences forgot about him because of the shock of finding out that his girlfriend was a man.

One of the things that disturbs me about a movie like *Boys Don't Cry* is that it works on dread, rather than suspense. It's a very primitive way to make a movie. I don't like movies that work on dread, and yet they're often taken very seriously because of that dread factor. You sit there knowing that this poor guy is going to be beaten to a pulp, and it's an awful feeling.

Earlier on, you mentioned *Magnolia*. Something I really like about it was Paul Thomas Anderson's use of Aimee Mann's music. Half the time it's being heard on someone's radio, the rest of the time it's understood to be playing in someone's brain.

Yes. Wasn't the music wonderful in the best movies of the seventies?

Martin Scorsese's movies, especially. But he seems to have lost that.

Scorsese was great, but now he's become kind of blah.

All of a sudden, he's gotten a tin ear.

His movies are terrible, and the music in them is terrible. I didn't see *Bringing Out the Dead*. It was the first one of his I didn't go to. But remember *Mean Streets*, when you heard the music?

Starting with "Be My Baby," yeah.

Wow.

In Anderson's *Boogie Nights*, it was "Jessie's Girl."

I liked *Boogie Nights*, the first half of it.

That scene where Alfred Molina is coked up and ranting, and holding a gun on everyone and singing along with Rick Springfield's "Jessie's Girl"—I don't know how anyone could hear that song again without remembering the mayhem of that scene. *Boogie Nights* and *Magnolia* are epics, in their way. They're Altmanesque.

They're big.

He's one of the few younger filmmakers I know of who can work on that large a scale without seeming pretentious or overextended.

I think you're right.

He's got something.

He does. I don't fully understand what he's up to, or know if he's up to anything yet. He might just be feeling his oats. But his movies are fun to watch. He has something. So does David O. Russell, and so many of the directors we hear about all the time don't, like — well, I guess the Coen brothers showed they did in *Raising Arizona*.

The only thing of theirs I've really liked was *The Big Lebowski* — I almost said *The Big Lewinsky*.

Now, that would be a title.

Jeff Bridges and John Goodman are both very good in it.

I haven't seen it. I'm behind on a couple of their films. But I'm fascinated by all the brother teams in movies now. It started with the Taviani brothers in Italy. Now there are so many brothers working together. I think it's because making a movie is so difficult and hair-raising that if you have somebody you can trust working alongside you, it makes a world of difference. The Coens, the Wachowskis, the Farrellys—it's one after another. I think for comedy it might be invaluable to have a brother or a sister. It's so hard to write a funny script. And to have someone who intuitively responds to what you do must be great.

Speaking of the Farrellys, have you seen *Me, Myself & Irene*?

Yes. It's very poor. It's a real disappointment, because I loved Jim Carrey.

I know you did. Did you see him as Andy Kaufman in *Man on the Moon*?

Yes. I thought he was fine, but the movie was so dismal—a terrible letdown. I saw Andy Kaufman perform a number of times, and he was more interesting than the movie made him out to be. There was no mystery in the film, as there was seeing him. I saw him a number of times without ever seeing that goddamn alter-ego, Tony Clifton, who occupies so much of the movie.

A problem I had with it was that Jim Carrey wants so desperately for us to like him, whereas Andy Kaufman seemed determined to make sure we wouldn't.

I read a section of the script in — *Vanity Fair*, I think it was. And it looked terrific, as if they really understood Andy Kaufman and could bring it off. But when I saw the movie, and saw that so much of it was centered on Tony Clifton, I couldn't believe they'd wasted such a great opportunity. I think that Milos Forman is totally the wrong director for the material. I'm not sure what material he would be the right director for, but this he just didn't get at all. And somehow or other, Jim Carrey's gifts worked to his disadvantage. He really is a loony comedian of a kind that I adore, and the only exciting comedian who's turned up in movies in the last few years. Don't you agree?

I guess so. But twenty years ago, you could look at the cast of *Saturday Night Live* and take your

pick. Now only Tim Meadows is occasionally funny.

He does have moments when he has that gleam in his eye. But of the ones who have gone into movies, who's kept it up? Bill Murray is wonderful from time to time. But who else is still really good?

Not Eddie Murphy.

No, definitely not Eddie Murphy. I went to see him in *Raw*, and it was the most unpleasant experience, being white in an otherwise black audience as he did his material. Everything that was wonderful about Richard Pryor, he made ugly and uncomfortable. With Richard Pryor, you applauded his genius, which transcended race. It was the essence of blackness, but he didn't make you feel awful about being white. When you saw Eddie Murphy with a black audience, you really sort of quivered in your boots.

I think Mike Myers has his moments. I especially liked the second *Austin Powers*.

And Mini-Me was a brilliant idea, although I don't know that he did as much with it as he might have.

I have to say, I don't get Adam Sandler at all. I don't understand what makes him funny to people. I laugh very easily, but I don't laugh at him.

I've never gotten him. Or Chris Farley, either.

I got Chris Farley a couple of times, but just a couple of times. The rest of the time his grossness was just appalling.

Adam Sandler, though, makes me wonder: If I were twenty-five years younger, would I think he was funny?

Would you?

I think not. But there are people who would say we're the problem—that it's an age thing.

Well, I don't think that's the problem. Some of the current women on the show aren't bad, but for the most part they're teammates to the men. They can be pretty funny, but the material they're given has a sourness to it.

Have you seen *Shaft*?

I haven't seen the new *Shaft*. I saw the old one. The new one is the Armani *Shaft*.

It's fun, though—like a comic book. And Samuel L. Jackson, I always enjoy watching.

I do, too. I especially liked him in that movie where he played a doctor, with all those beautiful black actresses—*Eve's Bayou*. Another good little movie that a lot of people don't know about.

Our mutual friend Carrie Rickey, the film critic for *The Philadelphia Inquirer*, was telling me that she thought that the new *Shaft*'s relative failure at the box office proves that Samuel L. Jackson isn't really a movie star in the conventional sense.

I don't believe that. I think that the audience is alert when he's on the screen, and that's all you can ask of an actor. I mean, they can't always triumph over their material. *Shaft* was rather tired material the first time around. It was the song that made it famous, I think.

This *Shaft* is more like Clint Eastwood's character in the *Dirty Harry* movies, or Mel Gibson's in the *Lethal Weapon* movies.

Did you see *Conspiracy Theory*, with Mel Gibson and Julia Roberts?

I missed it.

Mel Gibson is very good in it. In some ways, he gets better and better.

Except for *All About My Mother* and *Magnolia*, my favorite movie from last year was *Payback*. Did you see him in that?

I kept seeing the commercials for it, but I didn't see it.

It's a remake of *Point Blank*, based on a novel by Donald E. Westlake, one of the series he wrote about a hit man, under the pseudonym Richard Stark.

I like Donald Westlake. He writes some of the funniest book reviews that appear in the *Times*. I think he's awfully good, and I love his scripts, but I've had my fill of that kind of book. Movies satisfy that desire for me, for pulp. When I read, I want something where there's some real interest in the sentences, where there's something going on in them. And even the best pulps don't give me that. I read a lot of them when I was a kid, and I've read some of them with great pleasure as an adult—that one by David Goodis that *Shoot the Piano Player* was based on. That was pretty good. But I want something more now. Anyway, who else is in *Payback*?

David Paymer and Kris Kristofferson, among others, and a blonde named Maria Bello, in the Angie Dickinson role. It's terrific—very savvy about its genre, extremely violent and very, very funny. As long as you accept the fact that Gibson's character is unsavory and completely amoral, and you're not going to judge him by how nice a guy he really is, you're on his side. Partly because it's Mel Gibson and he's so charismatic. He also narrates, and nobody speaks American any better, or hard-boiled any better.

I'll see it. It's a great title.

How do you see movies at this point? At the local multiplex, with everybody else? Advance cassettes?

Both of those methods. A lot of directors whose work I was kind to send me videos when they have new pictures coming out. Surprisingly, so do a number of people whose work I was not kind to, because they want my opinion and they know I can't do them any harm now. That's a very funny development. I live in a community that has four screens, and they change pictures pretty quickly. So I get to see most things I want to. I find that I'm not really eager to see a lot of the films, and sometimes I have to prod myself to go see them. Most of them are bummers. They're the same ones playing across the country, because, of course, the movie companies discovered it was more economical to play movies all over at the same time so they can advertise them on television. So I see what my sisters in San Francisco see and what people around the country see.

It's like the scene in Truffaut's *Day for Night*, when the director and his crew want to go to the movies

and every theater is showing the same thing. But at least it's *The Godfather*, not *Gladiator*.

No, I wouldn't mind if they went on playing that for a few weeks. That's a wonderful movie. I'm thinking particularly of the second one, when you see how it fits in to the first, when Robert De Niro as the young Don Corleone walks the streets of old New York, and that sequence where he shoots the padrone—it's so brilliant, it's stupefying.

Do you miss having a biweekly forum to share your perceptions with readers?

Sharing is a nice way of putting it. I loved writing about things when I was excited about them. It's not fun writing about bad movies. I used to think it was bad for my skin. It's painful writing about the bad things in an art form, particularly when young kids are going to be enthusiastic about those things, because they haven't seen anything better or anything different. I mean, if you were writing about *The Perfect Storm*, you would have to consider that for many kids it's the first time they've ever seen something like that, and they're all excited about it, and all of their buttons have been pushed. They're going to be very angry if they read a review by someone who doesn't respond to it. I got a lot of that kind of mail from young moviegoers, high-school and college kids, who couldn't understand why I wasn't as excited about things like *The Towering Inferno* as they were. And there are *Towering Inferno*s coming out all the time. The people on television who got excited last week about *The Patriot* are getting excited this week about *X-Men*, and they'll get excited about something else next week. But if you write critically, you have to do something besides get excited. You have to examine what's in front of you. What you see is a movie industry in decay, and the decay gets worse and worse.

INDEX

༈